HELP! I'M TRAPPED IN THE FIRST DAY OF SUMMER CAMP

1

"Just be yourself," said my sister, Jessica.

"Just try your best," said my father.

"Just remember to brush your teeth," said my mother.

We were sitting in the kitchen, having breakfast. They were giving me advice before I went away to sleep-away camp for the first time.

"Thanks, guys, I'll remember all that." I yawned and stretched.

Mom narrowed her eyes and studied me closely. "You look tired. Didn't you sleep last night?"

"Sure, I did," I said, even though I'd hardly slept at all.

"No way," said Jessica. "He was up all night tossing and turning in bed. Can you believe the great Jake Sherman is scared about going away to camp for the first time?"

"Am not," I said.

"Are too," she shot back. "I know you, Jake. You're totally freaked."

"I don't see why he should be scared," Mom said. "After all, he's only going for a month and his two best friends will be there with him."

"But Camp Walton has a rule against friends sharing bunks," Jessica said. "Jake's little play pals Josh and Andy will be in other cabins."

"But they'll be at the same camp," Dad said, "'they'll get to see each other."

"Doesn't matter," my sister said. "What matters is who Jake shares his cabin with. What happens when they find out what a dork he is? What if they all hate him?"

"Hon?" said my mother to my sister.

"You guys never went to camp when you were kids," Jessica went on. "You don't have a clue how scary going for the first time can be. I mean, knowing Jake, he'll probably do something really dumb on the first day. What if he comes off looking like a fool? Once he's got that label, he's finished. Believe me, I'd be freaked too if I were Jake. This could turn out to be the worst summer of his life."

"*Ahem!*" Mom cleared her throat loudly. "Are you *sure* Jake needs to hear this?"

"Absolutely," Jessica insisted. "Don't you remember what happened to me on my first day at camp? I tripped during a ball game and got a face full of mud. For the rest of the summer they called me Mud Face. It was a total bummer. I hated it. If you ask me, I don't even know why they call it summer camp. Summer *prison* is more like it. It can be pure tor — "

"*Hon!*" Mom blurted. "Please stop now. You're scaring Jake."

Jessica blinked and looked surprised.

"Yeah," I said. "What do you want me to do? Stay home with you?"

Jessica's eyes widened. "No!"

Mom smiled. "I think Jessica just got a little carried away. I'm sure this is going to be a great month for Jake."

"It's definitely going to be a great month for me without my skinkbrain brother around," said Jessica.

"You may be surprised," said Mom. "You may actually discover you miss Jake."

"Right." Jessica smirked. "I may also discover that I have an extra eye growing out the back of my head and that I love eating chocolate-covered cockroaches, but somehow I doubt it."

My sister was going to spend the summer at the town pool being a junior lifeguard, whatever that meant.

"Listen, guys," I said. "I'm sure everything's going to be cool at Camp Walton, and I'm gonna have a great time."

"That's the spirit." Mom gave me an encouraging smile.

"Just remember, Jake," said my father, "even if you're completely miserable and unhappy, you have to stay. After the first week, they don't give refunds if you leave early. So no matter how bad it gets, you're stuck there."

Mom sighed at Dad. "I know you mean well, dear, but I'm not sure that's the most positive approach to take."

"Look, Mom, Dad," I said. "It really doesn't matter. I — "

Ding dong! The doorbell rang.

Groof! Groof! Lance, our yellow Labrador retriever, started barking.

Jessica got up, went to the kitchen window, and looked outside. "Oh, my gosh! You're not going to believe this!"

2

I went to the kitchen window. Outside my friends Alex Silver, Julia Saks, and Amber Sweeny were standing on the sidewalk in front of our house. They were holding up a large banner made out of a bed sheet. The banner said:

Have A Great Time At Camp

Don't Come Back

"I guess I'm not the only one who's not going to miss you," Jessica quipped.

"You're a real riot, Jess," I grumbled, and went to the front door.

As soon as I stepped outside, my friends reached into their pockets and pulled out giant handkerchiefs they must have torn from another sheet. They pretended to cry and blow their noses.

"Gee, guys," I said. "I didn't know you cared." "We don't," Alex said as he dabbed his eyes. "It must be an allergy or something."

Julia handed me a shoe box. "We took up a collection and got this for you."

"What is it?" I asked.

"A survival kit," said Amber.

I opened the box. Inside was a bag of party balloons, a can of Cheese Whiz, a pack of crackers, and a small box of Band Aids.

"I can understand the Cheese Whiz, crackers, and Band Aids," I said. "But what's with the balloons?"

"You can't survive camp without them," said Alex.

"What are you talking about?" I said.

"Balloons are an essential component in the manufacture of water balloons," he explained. "Camp without water balloons is like a Big Mac without fries."

"Thanks, I'll remember that." I slid the box under my arm. "You guys sure know how to make a kid feel good."

"So when do you leave?" Julia asked.

I checked my watch. "Any minute now."

Amber pointed at my T-shirt. "It's really called Camp Walton?"

"No," I said. "It's called Camp Big-Chewy-Booger but they ran out of those T-shirts so I have to wear this."

Julia and Amber grinned, but Alex had a pained expression on his face. "Seriously, Jake, what do you want to go to camp for?"

"I guess because I've never tried it," I said.

"You've never tried bungee jumping off the Golden Gate Bridge either," said Amber. "You gonna try that next?"

"Probably not," I said.

"So what are we supposed to do for the next month while you're gone?" Alex asked.

"Uh ... sit around and miss me?" I suggested.

"Fat chance." Julia smirked.

"Just remember, dude," Alex said. "New experiences can be dangerous. Look what happened to Icarus."

Amber frowned. "Who?"

"Don't you remember that Greek dude who made wings out of wax?" Alex asked. "He flew too close to the sun and the wax melted and he fell back to earth and did the big splat."

"If I make any wax wings in arts and crafts, I'll remember not to fly too close to the sun," I said.

Just then Dad, Mom, and Jessica came out.

"Time to go, Jake," said my father as he lugged my big green duffle bag to our van and dumped it in the back. The rear of the van dipped and the springs squeaked. Then Mom and Jessica got in.

My friends grew silent. It was time for me to leave. Suddenly I actually did start to feel a little nervous. Then I had an idea.

"Hey, you guys want to come with us to the place where the camp bus picks me up?" I asked.

"Not exactly the most exciting offer we've ever had," Alex muttered.

"Where it is, anyway?" asked Amber.

"The parking lot of Super Donut," I said.

"Would your parents get us some donuts if we went?" Julia asked.

"Uhh ... I don't see why not," I said.

My friends started to grin.

"Suddenly I want to be with Jake until the very last second," said Alex.

"Wait, Jake." My father rolled down his window and stuck his head out. "Don't forget we have to pick up Josh and Andy and all their stuff. That won't leave much room."

"Aw, darn, and I thought we were going to get something good out of this," Julia said with a sigh.

"Sorry, guys." I waved at my friends and got into the van. "Guess I'll see you when I get back."

3

We picked up Josh and Andy at their houses and threw their duffle bags in the van. My friends and I sat together in the back. They weren't exactly happy campers.

"I can't believe I'm going to this dumb camp," Josh groaned.

"Yeah," Andy agreed. "I mean, what's wrong with hanging around here and complaining that there's nothing to do? That's what we do every summer."

"Look, guys, this could be really good for us," I said.

"Really good for *you,* maybe," Josh grumbled. "Not for me. I'm the chubby kid. You ever notice in every camp movie there's a chubby kid with six candy bars in his pocket who can't make it around the bases without stopping to catch his breath. Well, that's me."

"No way," I said. "You're a good athlete."

"You and Andy know that," said Josh. "But no one else does. Everyone's gonna look at me and think of the chubby kid in those movies. They're never gonna give me a chance. I never should've told my parents you were going to camp. Then they wouldn't be making me go."

"Yeah." Andy nodded. "This really bites."

"What's your problem?" I asked him. "You're not chubby."

"I've got braces," Andy said.

"So?"

"So they're gonna give me a dumb nickname," Andy said. "Everybody gets a nickname in camp. Mine's gonna be something really stupid like railroad lips or terminator teeth."

"You guys worry too much," I said. "Camp Walton's going to be totally cool."

But Andy and Josh didn't look convinced.

"You guys know what a super-wedgy is?" Andy asked.

Josh and I shook our heads. "Never heard of it."

"My cousin told me about it," Andy explained. "They only have them at camps. The camp cabins have rafters. So they take a rope and put one end through your belt. The other end goes over the rafter. Then they haul you up."

"Eww!" Josh winced in imagined pain and reached for the van's door handle. "Forget it, I'm not going."

"Hold it, you guys," I said. "I think you're just nervous because they won't let us bunk together. But maybe that's good. We're always together, so this'll be different."

"Sure," Josh moaned. "We'll all get super-wedgied in a different cabin."

"I'll tell you what will be different," Andy said in a low voice so my parents and sister wouldn't hear. "Being away from Mr. Dorkson's dumb machine. At least we won't have to worry about switching bodies with anything for a while."

Josh pretended to look surprised. "Gee, Andy, I thought you liked being Jake's dog."

"Very funny," Andy replied sourly.

Just a few months before, Andy and my dog Lance had accidentally switched bodies. Lance, in Andy's body, went to regular school while Andy, in Lance's body, went to obedience school.

"So listen, guys," I said. "Did you get flashlights?"

"Oh, yeah." Josh opened his day pack and took out a long black flashlight. "It's made of aluminum. Not only does it work as a flashlight, but if I run into any bears in the woods, I can whack 'em on the head."

"Cool," I said, getting out my dual action light. "Mine not only has a spotlight. It has a wide-area fluorescent that blinks automatically so that if I get lost in the woods at night a search plane can find me."

We both turned to Andy, to see what kind of flashlight he'd gotten. Andy opened his day pack and took out a huge thing with a pistol grip and curly black cord leading to a separate battery pack.

"Oh, wow!" I gasped. "That's incredible."

Andy grinned sheepishly. "It's called the SuperBeam. One million candle power. Twenty-five times brighter than the high beams on this van. This thing could light up a whole baseball stadium."

Only Josh didn't look impressed. "It may be bright, but what good is that going to do if you run into a bear?"

"I'll just have to blind him," Andy replied with a smile.

4

The camp bus hadn't arrived yet when we got to the Super Donut. Mom, Dad, and Jessica went inside to buy donuts. Josh, Andy, and I hung out in the parking lot. Josh mumbled something under his breath.

"What?" I didn't quite catch what he'd said.

Josh and Andy winked at each other and grinned.

"What'd you say?" I asked. "I didn't get it."

"I said,' The fungus says, "What?"'" Josh spoke more clearly.

"What?" I said.

Josh and Andy grinned some more.

Then I got it and felt my face turn red. "Very funny, guys."

"But you have to admit it's a good one," Andy said.

"Yeah, right." I started to look around, scoping out the other campers.

"Check out those guys." Andy pointed at three kids throwing a baseball around on the other side of the parking lot. They could all throw really hard and far.

"Serious jock types," Josh said.

"The cool guys," Andy added warily. "Watch out."

"Maybe they're okay," I said.

"Sure, and maybe I'm the frog prince," Andy said. "They're too cool. That's why they're over there throwing the ball around. They want to make sure everyone sees them. You see any parents with them?"

Josh and I shook our heads.

"Of course not," Andy said. "They're letting everyone know that they're too cool to have parents. Not like the rest of us dweebazoids waiting around for the bus with Mom and Dad."

As Andy said that, he pointed at the kids who were waiting with their parents. In a weird way it seemed like he was right. The kids who hung with their parents did seem dorkier. Their clothes and hair didn't look as cool.

I looked back at the cool guys. They were definitely wearing the coolest clothes and sneakers, and they had the coolest hair. Then I compared my friends to them. Unfortunately it was hard for Josh to look cool because he was chubby and his face was always red. And Andy rarely looked cool because he had braces and a few zits.

Then I looked down at my own sneakers and clothes. I thought I looked pretty cool too. Could I fit in with those cool guys?

Mom, Dad, and Jessica came out of the Super Donut with three yellow and red travel boxes of donuts.

"There is one good thing about parents bringing you to the bus," I said. "They supply the donuts."

"You're right about that," Josh admitted and patted his day pack. "Sure beats Cheese Whiz on crackers."

Andy looked surprised. "You brought that too?" *

"So did I," I said.

"It's the universal emergency camp food," said Josh.

My parents and sister arrived with the donuts.

"How come so many boxes, Mrs. Sherman?" Andy asked, eyeing the donuts hungrily.

"We're going to take one box home with us," Mom replied. "The second box we'll eat here, and the third is for Jake to take on the bus and share with all his new friends."

Andy grinned and put his lips close to my ear. "You're going to share your donuts on the bus," he teased. "Aw, isn't that cute?"

"Drop dead." I gave him a poke with my elbow.

Meanwhile, Dad opened the first box of donuts. "Come and get 'em, boys."

Josh, Andy, and I each took a donut, then walked a dozen feet away and stood by ourselves.

"Is it my breath?" Dad asked with a concerned look.

As usual, brain-girl Jessica figured out the real reason. "No, Dad, it's Jake. He's afraid that if he stands with his parents he won't look cool to the other kids."

"Then maybe we should go," said Mom.

That made me feel bad.

"Naw, it's okay," I said. "You guys can stay."

"We can stay," said Jessica. "But we're not allowed to get too close to you, right?"

"Right." I nodded.

Jessica rolled her eyes. "Pathetic."

"Oh, look." Mom pointed at a family on the other side of the parking lot. "Isn't that the Peelings?"

We looked across the parking lot at a tall kid with glasses and black hair. He was wearing a white Camp Walton T-shirt and green-and-red-plaid shorts. Some lady, probably his mother, was making him stand still while she reached up and combed his hair.

"You're right," Dad said. "We haven't seen them in years."

"Now that I think of it, they had a boy the same age as Jake," said Mom. "Let's go say hello."

Mom and Dad walked across the parking lot. Meanwhile, the kid's mother was still combing his hair.

"Can you believe she's doing that in public?" Andy whispered.

"What's worse is that he's letting her do it," Josh added. "That kid must be a triple mega-dorkazoid."

We watched as my parents introduced themselves to the dorkazoid's parents. A few moments later, my mother turned and waved across the parking lot to me. "Jake, hon? Come on over. There's someone here we'd like you to meet."

"Tough break, Jake." Andy grimly clapped his hand on my shoulder. "You just became a dorkazoid by association."

As I walked slowly across the parking lot toward my parents and the Peelings, I glanced back at the cool kids playing ball, and hoped they weren't watching. Mr. Peeling was a tall, gawky-looking guy like his son. He had one of the longest necks and the biggest Adam's apple I'd ever seen, and sort of reminded me of a giraffe. Mrs. Peeling was a large woman with a big blond hairdo and lots of jewelry around her neck and wrists. Definitely more of a hippo.

I could just imagine what the son of a giraffe and hippo would be like. Definitely not cool.

"Jake," Mom said, "I want you to meet Mr. and Mrs. Peeling and their son, Peter. They used to be our neighbors in the city. We just found out that you and Peter are both in cabin B-13. Isn't that wonderful?"

Peter held out his hand. It was pretty limp, and he had awful long fingernails for a boy. He didn't look at me when we shook hands.

"Oh, I think this is sooo wonderful!" Mrs. Peeling gushed. "Petey's been sooo worried that he wouldn't know anyone at camp. We had to force him to go. If it was up to him, he'd just sit in front of the TV all day and —"

"Uh, Mom," Peter interrupted. He had a pained look on his face. "I really don't think you have to tell them all that."

"Why not Petey?" his mom asked. "It's true, isn't it?"

Peter's face turned red and I felt bad for him. His mother sure wasn't helping things by embarrassing him like that.

"This is your lucky day, Petey," Mr. Peeling said. "Jake looks like a nice boy. I'm sure you two are going to be best friends by the time camp is over."

An awkward moment passed while neither Peter nor I knew what to say. Just then I happened to look down at his feet. Peter was wearing sandals. He had the longest toenails I'd ever seen.

They were almost lethal weapons!

I straightened up. Peter might have been the greatest guy on earth, but there was no way I was going to be friends with anyone who wore sandals and had killer toenails.

We all heard the squeak of brakes. A green bus pulled into the parking lot. It looked like an old school bus that had been repainted.

"We better go get your stuff, Jake," Dad said. He and Mom said good-bye to the Peelings.

Peter and I just nodded at each other.

"So what do you think of Peter?" Mom asked in a low voice as we walked back across the parking lot to the car.

"I don't know, Mom. He seems a little geeky."

"You'd be geeky too if you had Margaret Peeling for a mother," my father whispered.

"John!" Mom gasped under her breath. "That's not very nice."

"Well, maybe not, but it's the truth, isn't it?" Dad replied with a shrug.

Mom didn't answer. She turned to me. "Well, anyway, Jake. Since he's in th same cabin as you, it would be very nice if you two became friends."

"Sure, Mom," I said. But inside I was thinking, *No way!*

We got back to the van. All around us, parents were giving their kids last minute instructions. Or hugging them. Or, in Peter Peeling's case, combing his hair again. The three cool baseball players carried their duffle bags toward the bus. Their parents were nowhere in sight.

Mom spread her arms. "Can I give you a hug and a kiss good-bye, Jake?"

"Uh ..." I took a step back and looked around, hoping that the cool guys weren't watching.

"Get with the program, Mom." Jessica smirked. "Cool kids don't even *have* mothers. As far as Jake's concerned, you've ceased to exist."

Mom gave me a crooked smile and dropped her arms.

Dad held out his hand. "Then how about a manly shake?"

"Sure." I shook his hand.

"Put 'er there, Jake." Jessica held out her hand. I shook it.

Mom sighed and held out her hand as well. "I'm glad we can conclude this meeting in a businesslike manner," she said sarcastically as we shook. "Just don't forget to brush your teeth."

"Sure, Mom."

Josh and Andy had already gotten on the bus. I got my day pack and duffle bag out of the van. The day pack contained my flashlight, Discman, some CDs, and a bag of chips for the bus ride. The duffle bag weighed a ton.

As I trudged toward the bus, almost bent double by the weight of the duffle, Josh opened a window and stuck his head out. "What's in that thing?"

"Don't know. My mom packed it." With a grunt I heaved the duffle bag onto the luggage carrier welded to the back of the bus.

"Better hurry," Josh said. "Looks like you're the last one to get on."

He was right. All the other campers were already on the bus. I spun around to my parents and sister and gave them one last wave. "See you in a month."

"No rush," Jessica called back. She waved with her right hand. Her left hand was behind her back.

I climbed onto the bus. The doors closed behind me and the bus lurched into motion. As I looked out the window, Jessica brought her left hand from behind her back. She held up a red and yellow box of donuts.

My donuts!

Jessica rubbed her stomach and licked her lips. She'd stolen my donuts!

That slimeball!

The bus started to move. I was still standing in the front. I looked at the rows of faces in the seats. A lot of the kids were younger, a few were my age and a few were older. Some of them looked back at me. Others gazed out the windows. Still others were already talking to the kid they were sitting next to.

"You better get a seat, son," said an older guy, who was sitting right behind the bus driver. He was wearing glasses, a gray Camp Walton T-shirt, and holding a clipboard.

"Yo, Jake!" About halfway back, Andy waved at me. He was sitting next to Josh. I walked down the aisle toward them. As I got nearer I saw that the closest empty seat was in the row behind them, right next to ... Peter Peeling.

Dork by association... Andy's words echoed in my ears. Part of me said "Don't sit there," but another part of me remembered what Mom had said about being nice. Sitting with the guy on the bus couldn't hurt, could it?

I stopped next to Peter. He looked up at me and smiled a little.

I was just about to sit down in the seat next to him when a voice said, "Look out."

I followed the voice to the back of the bus. The three cool baseball players were sitting in the last row, watching me. They were all wearing headphones, listening to iPods, and munching on Pringles.

"You really want to sit there?" one of them asked. He was short and stocky, with short black hair and a diamond stud in one ear.

I hesitated and looked down at Peter. He quickly looked away. His ears and cheeks were growing red.

"Hey, it's a free country," said another one of the cool guys in a mocking tone. He was the tallest of the three and had bushy blond hair.

"Yeah, but you gotta watch out for cooties," said the short guy.

The third guy said nothing. His hair was longer and light brown. He was wearing a leather thong around his neck with a single large bead in it.

Andy and Josh twisted around in their seat and looked at me with puzzled expressions.

"Aren't you going to sit?" Andy asked.

"Back there," I answered, and sat down in an empty row halfway between Peter Peeling and the cool guys.

"Definitely a wise decision," said the short stocky guy with the earring.

"So what's your name?" asked the guy with the longer brown hair and the leather thong.

"Jake," I said. "What's yours?"

"Rick," the kid said.

"Dan," said the stocky kid with the dark hair.

"Zack," said the blond guy. "What cabin you in?"

"B-13," I said. "You?"

"The very same," said Rick, and the other two nodded to show they were in at cabin also.

"Should be a pretty cool group this year," said Dan.

"With one definite exception," added Zack, looking past me at Peter.

The bus went over a bump and I felt my eyes open. For a second I didn't know where I was. Then I realized I'd fallen asleep. I yawned and looked out the window. We were pulling into a big gravel parking lot. Other buses were already there and kids wearing white Camp Walton T-shirts were climbing out of them.

In the parking lot, older guys wearing gray Camp Walton T-shirts and carrying clipboards were talking to small groups of campers. In the background were some buildings made of brown logs, and behind them was a lake with a dock and some sailboats.

I rubbed my eyes and stretched.

"Have a nice nap, Sleeping Beauty?" someone asked.

I looked up into Zack's smiling face as he, Dan, and Rick filed down the aisle past me.

"Oh, yeah." I stretched and yawned again.

"See ya in the cabin," said Rick.

A moment later they passed Peter Peeling as he stood up. He picked up a white paper shopping bag that must have contained his bus stuff. The rest of us had day packs. The shopping bag was like Peter — hopelessly dorky.

"Cool bag," Zack said with a chuckle.

Peter didn't reply. He just bowed his head and wouldn't look Zack in the eye. He waited until they left the bus. When they were gone, he went down the aisle and got off.

That left three people on the bus: Josh, Andy, and me.

"How come you didn't sit with us?" Josh asked.

"Uh, well, I knew I was gonna sleep," I lied.

"Bull," Andy said. "You just didn't want to sit next to that Peeling kid. So, did you make friends with the cool guys?"

"Not really," I said, getting up.

"Well, there's still plenty of time," Andy said, as if he could read my mind.

Andy, Josh, and I went down the aisle. Outside the bus, the driver was pulling the duffle bags out of the luggage carrier. Peter Peeling got his bag and spoke to an older guy wearing a grey Camp Walton T-shirt. The guy checked his clipboard, then pointed toward a line of small wooden buildings, which must have been the cabins where we campers would live.

I saw the driver pull out my duffle bag and drop it to the ground with a thud. I went over and struggled to pick it up. Rick, Dan, and Zack were still waiting for theirs.

"What'd you put in there?" Dan, the stocky kid with the black hair, asked with a smile. "Bowling balls?"

I almost answered that I didn't know what was in the bag because my mom had packed for me. But I caught myself. Admitting your mom packed for you wasn't cool.

"I listen to a lot of heavy metal," I said.

Dan scowled, but Rick grinned. He was the one with the brown hair.

"*Heavy* metal?" he said. "That's funny. Are you a comedian?"

"Only when I'm awake," I said.

By now, Andy and Josh had gotten their duffle bags.

"So where's your cabin?" Andy asked me.

I pointed toward B-13.

"Bummer," he said. "Josh and I are that way." He pointed toward some cabins on the other side of a large field with some soccer goals and a baseball diamond.

"Guess I'll catch you guys later," I said, and started to lug my duffle bag toward my cabin.

Halfway to the cabin, Rick, Dan and Zack passed me. Their duffle bags looked a lot lighter.

"Come on, Sleeping Beauty, don't be such a slowpoke," Zack teased. He was the tall one with the bushy blond hair. I struggled to keep up with them. Ahead we could see Peter Peeling carrying his duffle and white shopping bag. All of a sudden the bottom of the shopping bag split and all the stuff inside spilled onto the grass. Peter dropped his duffle and started to pick up the items, which included a white plastic thing with a long, clear plastic tube attached to it.

Zack, Rick, and Dan paused to watch.

"Hey, guys, look," Zack said. "A Water Pik."

"Whoa." Dan grinned. "This guy takes serious care of his teeth."

"It's for my gums," Peter tried to explain.

"Gums, huh?" chuckled Dan. "Hey, maybe we should call him Gummi Bear."

"Yeah, that sounds right," agreed Zack. He turned to me. "What do you think, Sleeping Beauty?"

Suddenly the cool guys and Peter were looking at me, waiting for my reply. Peter winced at the nickname. I could just imagine him writing home and complaining that I'd agreed to call him Gummi Bear. His mother would probably call my mother and scream at her. But I wouldn't have to deal with that until I got home from camp. Right now I was just trying to survive the first fifteen minutes.

"Sounds okay to me." I shrugged and didn't look at Peter.

"So be it," Zack said. "See you in the cabin, *Gummi Bear*."

The cool guys started toward the cabin. I glanced at Peter, but he wouldn't look at me.

"Hey, Sleeping Beauty!" Dan yelled back to me. "You coming or what?"

"Uh, yeah, I'm coming," I said, and followed.

Our cabin was pretty small. First you went up two wooden steps to a porch, and then inside through a creaking screen door. Three double decker bunk beds stood in the middle and back. A regular bed was placed near the screen door.

"That's for the counselor," Dan said. "We get the double deckers."

Thunk! I dropped my duffle bag next to the first double decker I came to.

"You don't want to take that one, Sleeping Beauty," Zack said. "Only the weebs want to be close to the counselor."

"Come on back here with us," said Rick. "You can take the top of my bunk."

I dragged my duffle bag back to Rick's bunk bed and started to unpack. The bunks had thin mattresses, made up with white sheets and gray blankets.

The next camper to enter the cabin was Peter, who put his stuff down on the bunk nearest the counselor's bed.

"It never fails," Zack said in a low voice. Dan smiled.

The last kid in the cabin was small and blond with a slight build. The only bed left was the top of Peter's double decker, and without a word the blond kid took it.

"It never fails?" Dan said it like a question this time and looked at Zack. I knew he was asking if Zack thought the blond kid was a dweeb, too. I was starting to get the feeling that Zack was the ringleader.

"Looks like it," Zack replied. He looked at me. "What do you think, Sleeping Beauty?"

Every time they spoke to me, I felt like I was being tested. Part of me thought it was stupid, but another part of me really wanted to pass the test.

"It's your call," I said with a shrug.

It took a while to get everything unpacked. The reason my duffle bag was so heavy was that my mother had packed enough underwear for me to change four times a day for a month and still have some left over.

While I shoved underwear in my cubby, the cool guys asked where I was from and I asked where they were from. But there was another question I really wanted to ask. Finally I got up the nerve.

"It seems like you guys are pretty good friends," I said. "I thought they had a rule against friends sharing cabins."

"It's not a real firm rule," Zack said. "If you get your parents to write a letter saying you might not come back if you can't be with your friends, the camp overlooks it really fast."

I wished I'd known that sooner. I would have given anything to be with Josh and Andy. Then I wouldn't have to worry about making new friends or being singled out as a dweeb.

A tall, lanky older guy with curly black hair came in. He was wearing a gray Camp Walton T-shirt, and said his name was Marty and that he was our counselor. He had an easygoing smile and looked pretty friendly. But when he focused on Zack, Dan, and Rick his expression changed.

"Don't I remember you three from last year?" Marty asked. "Didn't you three bunk together?"

"So?" Zack asked back.

It looked like Marty was going to say something, but he just shrugged and told the rest of us to introduce ourselves. That's how I found out the small blond kid's name was Lewis.

Marty showed us how the cabin worked. Outside was a clothesline where we could hang our wet bathing suits and damp towels to dry, and in back of the cabin was a hose for washing down our tennis shoes and anything else that got muddy.

Then Marty said he had to go down to the waterfront because he was also one of the swimming instructors. He said he'd come back later and take us over to the cafeteria for lunch. In the meantime we should finish unpacking and get to know each other. He added that there was a new tetherball game in the front of the cabin and we could play if we wanted.

After Marty left, Zack strolled to the front of the cabin and looked up at Lewis. The small blond kid was kneeling on his bunk, tacking pictures of racing cars to a rafter over his bed.

"Guess you're into cars, huh?" Zack asked.

Lewis nodded.

"*Small* cars, right?" Zack said.

"*Fast* cars," Lewis replied.

"*Small* fast cars, then," said Zack with a grin.

In the back of the cabin Dan snickered.

Lewis looked down at Zack, right into his eyes. "You think you're funny?"

Zack blinked. Lewis was challenging him, which was kind of interesting considering Zack was at least eight inches taller and probably weighed forty pounds more.

"Whoa, tough little guy," Dan said in a low voice.

"Mighty Mouse," said Zack with a smile. "Yeah, that's what we're gonna call you. So we got Mighty Mouse and Gummi Bear in the first bunk."

Lewis turned back to his pictures and didn't say a word. Meanwhile, Peter had been sitting on the lower bunk, quietly unpacking his stuff.

Now Zack turned to him. "Hey, Gummi Bear, wanna play some tetherball?"

Every time one of the cool guys spoke to Peter, he seemed to shiver slightly. He always bowed his head, and never looked them in the eye.

"Uh, I'm not sure."

Zack put his hands on his hips. "What are you, some kind of wuss?"

In the back, Dan snickered again. I noticed that Rick was silent and didn't join his friends when they picked on kids.

"I ... I don't know what tetherball is," Peter said.

"How can you not know what tetherball is?" Zack asked in disbelief.

"Maybe they don't have it where he comes from," Rick said.

"Well, I'll show you," Zack said.

Peter's eyes darted around nervously. It was obvious he didn't want to play. "Uh, well, I haven't finished unpacking. Marty said we had to finish unpacking before we — "

"What's wrong with you?" Zack asked sharply. "You gonna listen to everything your counselor tells you?"

"Well — " Peter stammered.

"Bet I could beat you with one hand behind my back," Zack sneered.

"And on one foot," Dan added.

"Yeah," said Zack. "So how about it, Gummi Bear? Or do we have to start calling you Gummi *Chicken*?"

10

Peter, Zack, Dan, Rick, and I went out to the tetherball court. Lewis, still in the cabin, didn't seem interested in watching the game.

The ball was about the size of a volleyball. It was attached to a rope, and the other end of the rope was attached to the top of a tall metal pole stuck in the ground. The idea was to hit the ball with your fist and make it go around the pole while your opponent tried to make it go in the opposite direction.

Peter and Zack got into position around the tetherball pole.

"You start, Gummi Bear," Zack said, swinging the ball to Peter. Then Zack put his left hand behind his back and raised his left foot off the ground so that he was standing on one foot.

Peter punched the ball. As it swung around the pole, Zack launched himself the air and belted it with all his might. *Whap!* The ball whipped back around the pole so fast that Peter just barely managed to duck out of the way. As the ball sailed back to Zack, he smacked it again, and then again. The ball rocketed around the pole and reached the end of the tether in no time.

Zack won on one foot with one hand behind his back.

Except for the first time he hit it, Peter never touched the ball again.

Zack grinned triumphantly. Peter trudged into the cabin with his head hanging. Zack had made him look really bad.

"What a dweeb," Dan muttered contemptuously. "And did you see those toenails?"

Zack nodded. "The guy's hopeless." Then he focused on me. "How about you, Sleeping Beauty? Think *you* can beat me?"

11

I didn't really want to play Zack and lose. But losing would be better than chickening out. Then again, I didn't want to lose the way Peter lost — never even touching the ball. That wasn't any good either because it would make me look like a wuss. So not only would I have to play, but I'd have to put my body between Zack and the ball, which might cause serious damage to my head.

Given a choice between suffering serious damage to my head or being labeled a chicken wuss, I had to go with the damage.

Taking a deep breath and bracing myself to the prospect of impending pain, I stepped up to the tetherball.

Then I picked up my left leg and put my left arm behind my back. My heart was pounding and my mouth felt dry.

"Whoa!" Rick grinned.

"You don't have to do that," said Zack.

"Hey, I just want to give you an even chance," I replied with a smile.

"All right!" Rick laughed. "This guy's got guts."

"He's still gonna get obliterated," said Dan.

Zack squinted at me, as if wondering if I was really a threat. Then he grinned. "Okay, wise guy, you start."

I steadied the ball with my right hand and prepared to punch it. In my mind was a vision of the ball streaking back at me at supersonic speed and knocking me out cold.

"Hey, guys, time for lunch," someone said. We turned and saw our counselor, Marty, coming toward us. "Where are the others?"

"Still in the cabin," I replied, glad to get out of playing Zack in one-handed, one-footed tetherball.

A few moments later we all started walking toward the dining hall. As I walked with Zack, Rick, and Dan, I noticed that Lewis and Peter followed a dozen yards behind, talking quietly.

What could they be talking about? I wondered. Was Lewis advising Peter to stand up to Zack the way he had?

Meanwhile, the cool guys were also talking quietly.

"You bring the plastic wrap?" Zack asked Dan in a low voice.

"Got it right here." Dan patted his pocket. "Who're we gonna do it to?"

"Guess?" Zack jerked his head back toward Peter.

"Who's gonna do it?" Dan asked. Zack's eyes settled on me. "Sleeping Beauty, who else?"

12

The dining hall was in a big log cabin with a low ceiling. It was noisy and crowded. I spotted Josh and Andy, and we met to compare notes.

"How's your cabin?" I asked Josh.

"Okay," he said with a shrug.

"What about yours?" Andy asked me. "How's it going with the cool guys and Peter the dork?"

"They're really giving him grief," I said.

"You standing up for him?" Andy asked.

"Well, er..."

"Forget I even asked." Andy shook his head with disgust. "You're probably too worried about being labeled a dork yourself."

Just then a portly, bald man wearing a gray Camp Walton T-shirt picked up a microphone and told us all to sit. I went back to the table where the guys from B-13 were sitting. The only seat left was next to Peter. Marty sat on Peter's other side and Lewis was sitting across from him.

The portly man's name was Mr. Mailer. He was the owner of the camp. Over the microphone, he told how glad he was that we were all there, how much fun we'd have, and what a big happy family we'd be.

Peter had twisted around in his seat to listen.

Under the table, Zack slipped something into my hand. It was a round piece of plastic wrap.

"Put it over Gummi Bear's glass," he whispered.

It didn't even occur to me to refuse. I reached over and silently stretched the plastic wrap over the top of Peter's glass.

"Make it really smooth so he doesn't notice," Dan added in a hushed voice.

When I was finished, I looked up and straight into the eyes of Lewis, who'd watched the whole thing. I waited for him to say something, or even tell Peter what I'd done. But he just gave me an inscrutable look, and then looked away.

When Mr. Mailer's welcoming speech ended, everyone turned back to the table. The camp waiters were coming out of the kitchen with big trays of food. Meanwhile, Zack reached for a metal pitcher in the middle of the table. "Who wants bug juice?"

"Me, me, me, me." Everyone at the table said they wanted some.

"Here you go." Zack stood up and poured out the bug juice. He held the pitcher high so that a long red stream cascaded out and into each glass.

Finally every glass except Peter's was filled.

"So, Gummi Bear, you sure you want some?" Zack asked.

Peter nodded.

"Bombs away." Zack poured.

The red bug juice hit the plastic wrap over Peter's glass and splattered in very direction. Most of it landed on Peter's T-shirt. The rest dripped off the table d into his lap, staining his shorts. In no time Peter's clothes were drenched in red.

"Gee, how'd that happen?" Zack scratched his head and pretended to be zzled.

Peter looked down at the plastic-covered glass, and then at Marty, our unselor, sitting on his left. Then he looked at Lewis sitting across from him. en at me, sitting on his right. We were the closest to him, so it made sense that e of us had put the plastic wrap on his glass.

Obviously Marty wouldn't have done it, and Peter had already made friends th Lewis. Peter's eyes stopped on me, and he stared with a hurt, defeated pression.

He knew I'd done it.

13

Peter went back to the cabin to change his clothes.

Marty gave Zack and Dan a stern look. "Yeah, now I remember. You guys really caused grief in your cabin last year. I'm surprised they let you bunk together again this year."

"Must've been a clerical error," Zack said with a shrug.

"Yeah, right." Marty wasn't fooled. "Try to give Peter a break, okay? You guys can all have a fine time this month without making him miserable, understand?"

We all nodded somberly. But when Marty looked away, Zack cracked a smile and winked.

The waiters served us lunch. Everyone stared down at their plates, but nobody lifted a fork. It was hard to tell exactly what lunch was. It was a glob of red and yellow with bits of green. Looking closely I identified noodles, cheese, and tomato sauce.

"Oh, man, not on the first day," Marty groaned, pressing his face into his hands.

"Yeah, this is no fair," Dan agreed. "They usually wait a few weeks before they hit us with this."

"What is it?" I asked.

"They call it American Chop Suey," Marty said unhappily. "Macaroni and cheese, broccoli, and whatever else happens to be lying around in the kitchen. Then they drown the whole thing in tomato sauce. Don't get the wrong idea, guys. This is a good camp. But the food stinks."

Nobody took more than two bites of the stuff. Lunch became bread, bug juice, and ice cream for dessert. I could have killed Jessica for stealing my donuts.

Afterwards, Marty gave us a tour of the camp, showing us the sports fields, the waterfront, and where the nature walk began. Then we had free time until dinner. Peter and Lewis went their separate ways. I found myself at the basketball court with Rick, Zack, and Dan.

Zack put his hands on his hips and looked around. "Too bad Gummi Bear's not here. It would be kind of fun to play some ball with him. Anyone know where he went?"

"I thought he said something about the nature walk," Rick said.

Zack grinned. "Figures. What about Mighty Mouse?"

"The waterfront," said Dan.

"Why don't the four of us play?" Rick suggested. "We can play two-on-two."

"You play B-ball, Sleeping Beauty?" Zack asked.

"A little," I replied cautiously.

"A little, huh?" Zack said. "Well, then you can be on Rick's team."

So Rick and I teamed up against Dan and Zack to play 21. We played half-court and the game stayed pretty close. Zack was a good basketball player, but Dan wasn't. Rick and I were a more balanced team.

Soon the score was tied 20-20. We were breathing hard. Our wet T-shirts clung to our sweaty bodies and our hair was plastered down with perspiration.

"Next basket wins," Rick reminded us.

Zack paused for a moment and whispered something in Dan's ear.

"Watch out," Rick cautioned me in a low voice. "They're cooking up a plan."

Dan started with the ball and I covered him. Somewhere behind me I could hear the scrape of basketball shoes against the pavement as Zack and Rick jockeyed for position.

Dan drove to my right. As soon as I started to follow, I tripped over something.

The next thing I knew, I was falling.

Wham! I hit the ground, scraping my hands and knees on the asphalt. Now I knew what had happened. Zack had stuck out his leg so that when Dan started his drive, I'd trip.

Meanwhile Zack spun around and took a pass from Dan. He went in for an easy lay-up and won the game.

"All right!" He and Dan shared a triumphant high five. They were both grinning.

I got up and dusted the dirt off my hands. "Nice trip, Zack."

The smile slowly disappeared from Zack's face. "What'd you say, Sleeping Beauty?"

"You tripped me," I said.

"I did not," Zack said. "You fell."

"Give me a break." I rolled my eyes.

Zack's eyes became beady. "What are you gonna do about it? Go cry to Marty like Gummi Bear would?"

"No," I said.

Zack grinned like he knew he had me, then turned away. It made me mad.

"The cretin says, 'What?' " I muttered in a low voice.

"What?" Zack stopped and looked back at me. The lines between his eyes made a deep V. Rick grinned. I could see he got it.

"Nothing," I said.

Zack turned away. "Come on, guys," he said to Dan and Rick. "Let's go."

Dan quickly started toward the cabin with Zack, but Rick stayed behind.

"Hey, come on," he said to me. "It was just a game."

I was still ticked off, but I realized what Rick was doing. He was giving me the chance to keep hanging with the cool guys. I couldn't say no.

Everybody met at the cabin before dinner. After the basketball game I was

eling pretty ripe, so I took a shower. When I came out of the bathroom, Zack had

ken off his shirt and draped a towel over his shoulder. I figured he was waiting to

ke a shower next. In the meantime, he was giving Peter grief again.

"You went on the *nature walk?"* Zack made a face. "What are you, some

nd of freak?"

Peter bowed his head and stared at the floor.

"Hey, Zack ..." Rick started to say.

"Yeah, what?" Zack snapped.

"Maybe you should leave the guy alone," Rick said.

"Guy?" Zack stared straight at Peter. "I don't see a guy. I don't know what I

e. It's like something from another planet."

Rick didn't answer. For some reason he looked at me.

"The dirtbag says, 'What?' " I muttered.

Zack spun toward me. "What?"

"Shower's free," I said.

Zack forgot about Peter and went into the bathroom. I caught Rick's eye. He

nked.

That night after dinner they were showing Pirates of the Caribbean in the dining hall. In the cabin before the movie, I saw Zack and Dan talking in low voices and knew they were planning something. Then Dan went into the bathroom.

"Everyone ready?" Marty asked.

"Dan's in the bathroom," Zack said.

"Okay, we'll wait," Marty said.

Dan took forever. After a while, Marty got impatient and walked to the back of the cabin.

"Hey, Dan, you okay?" he called into the bathroom.

"Yeah, I'll be out in a second," Dan called back.

"You sure you're not lost?" Zack yelled and everyone laughed. That was the thing about Zack. Not only was he cool and a good athlete, but he could be funny too.

When he wasn't being mean.

Dan finally got out of the bathroom and we headed toward the dining hall. I was looking forward to sitting with Josh and Andy, but when we got there it was dark inside. The movie had already started.

"Looks like we'll have to sit in the last row," Marty said in a hushed voice.

I had a feeling Zack and Dan had planned it that way. In the meantime, Marty didn't sit down with us.

"Okay, guys, you stay here and watch," he whispered. "I'll be back just before the movie's over." Then he left.

"Where's he going?" I whispered to Rick.

"Probably to hook up with the other counselors and figure out how to meet the counselors from the girls' camp across the lake," Rick whispered back.

We started to watch Pirates of the Caribbean, even though you had to assume every camper there had already seen it about a hundred times. After about ten minutes, I felt someone nudge my shoulder. Looking over, I saw Zack, Dan, and Rick sliding out of our row.

"You coming?" Zack whispered.

I hesitated. Marty had told us not to leave the movie.

But if I didn't... I was a dweeb.

I didn't ask any questions as we walked through the moonlight back toward the cabin. Crickets chirped in the dark and the night air was fresh and cool. Inside the cabin it was dark, but just enough moonlight came through the windows to allow us to see.

"No lights, guys," Zack whispered, then turned to me. "Hey, Sleeping Beauty, you know how to short-sheet a bed?"

I shook my head.

"Show him, Rick," Zack said as he picked up Peter's Water Pik and shined a small pencil flashlight on it.

Rick pulled the blanket off Peter's bed and started to show me what to do. "See, you double the sheet up short," he said. "Then the guy gets in and can't get his legs straight. We do it to everybody at least once. It's pretty harmless."

"What about Mighty Mouse?" Dan asked.

Zack looked up from the Water Pik and thought for a second. He shook his head. "Let's just do Gummi Bear tonight. Dan, you pull his springs."

While Rick and I doubled over the sheet so that it only went halfway down the bed, Dan crawled underneath. I heard the scrape and squeak of metal as he pulled out some of the springs that supported the mattress. Meanwhile, Zack got a small bottle of liquid detergent and poured it inside the Water Pik.

Dan crawled out from under Peter's bed with a handful of large gray springs. "Man, this is gonna be great! I bet Gummi Bear'll be packed up and gone by the morning."

Rick and I looked at each other. I wondered what he was thinking. Was the point to make Peter so miserable that he'd leave camp?

Rick and I finished. The truth was, I didn't feel good about doing it. Short-sheeting the bed might not be so bad. But the stuff Zack and Dan were doing was mean. Still, I was certain I'd be labeled a geek if I didn't go along with them. And then Zack might start goofing on me, too.

"What else can we do to Gummi Bear?" Dan asked.

Zack started to look around the cabin. But just then Rick walked to the door and peaked out.

"Hey, you hear that?" he whispered to us.

"What?" Zack whispered back.

"I think someone's coming!" Rick hissed.

Everyone froze. Zack tiptoed to the door and looked out. "I don't see anyone," he said in a low voice.

"Well, I thought I saw someone," Rick whispered.

Zack turned back to Dan and me. "Okay, guys, we better get back to the movie."

We quietly snuck out into the dark. No one was outside. I started to wonder if Rick had really seen someone or not. Or was that just his way of stopping Zack and Dan from doing anything more to Peter?

15

We snuck back into the dining hall and watched the end of the movie. Just before the lights went on, Marty rejoined us.

"Okay, guys," he said as the lights went back on, "what do you say we hit the canteen and then head back to the cabin?"

We walked over to the canteen, which was mobbed with campers who had the same idea as us. We got our ice cream, then I spotted Josh and Andy in the crowd and joined them.

"Hey, it's the cool guy," Josh said when he saw me.

"What are you talking about?" I asked.

"We heard about that stunt you pulled on Peter at lunch," Andy said. "You're just too cool for words, Jake."

"Yeah, you're our hero," Josh said snidely.

"Look, forget about it, okay?" I said. "I didn't know he was going to get splattered with bug juice. And anyway, I thought you guys said Peter was a dork."

"Maybe he is," said Andy. "But we wouldn't go out of our way to make his life miserable."

"Not like someone we know," added Josh.

"Okay, okay, I get the message," I said. "But how's it going with you guys? Meet anyone in your cabins that you like?"

Andy shrugged his shoulders. "I've spotted a few possible candidates, but n taking my time."

"I found a kid in my cabin I like," Josh said. "He's an overweight tubazoid ke me. I figure we'll stick together and fight off the cool guys who try to pick on ."

His words stung.

"And speaking of cool guys, how's it going with *you?"* Andy asked.

"All I'm doing is trying to get by, okay?" I said, feeling defensive. "No one ants to be labeled a dork, right?"

"Sure, Jake," Andy said. "Just don't forget, when in doubt, always pick on meone dorkier than you."

I left them and rejoined Marty and the guys, who were walking back to the bin with their ice creams. Talk about a shock — Zack was having a friendly chat th Peter!

"So, do they call tetherball something else where you come from?" Zack ked.

"Not really," replied Peter. "It never had a name. It was just the game with e ball on the rope. Like soap on a rope."

"Like soap on a rope!" Zack grinned. "That's a good one, Peter."

Peter smiled proudly. He was probably feeling really good because it looke

like the cool guys were finally accepting him.

Of course, he didn't know what lay ahead.

16

We got back to the cabin and Marty told us to get ready for bed. Zack had already warned us to stall so that Peter would be the first to use the bathroom.

The rest of us pretended to be busy. Peter was humming to himself, obviously in a good mood. Probably because he thought the cool guys liked him and camp wouldn't be so bad after all. Finally, he got his Water Pik and went into the bathroom. Zack quickly motioned for us to follow.

We couldn't get too close because Peter would see us in the mirror, so we huddled outside the bathroom and listened.

The Water Pik started to whir. Peter was still humming to himself. The humming and whirring sort of mixed together as he started to clean his teeth. But they were quickly joined by a third *spritzing* sound. Like whipped cream squirting out of a can.

"Huh? Wha . . . ?" Peter sounded like he was trying to talk through a mouthful of food. We heard him spit and gasp, "Hey! What's going on?"

I felt someone prod me from behind. It was Zack, pushing us into the bathroom. Peter saw us in the mirror and spun around. His mouth was covered with foam and it dribbled down his chin. Meanwhile, the Water Pik was spitting out a thin stream of foam over everything in sight!

Zack and Dan started falling all over themselves with laughter. Rick and I were more restrained, but we had to grin. It was a pretty funny sight.

The lines in Peter's forehead deepened as he wiped the foam away from his mouth. His dream of a great month of summer camp was going up in smoke.

Then Marty came into the bathroom. Everyone tensed as we waited to see how he'd react.

When our counselor saw what happened he just shook his head and smiled. "Don't worry, Peter. It's a practical joke. We always get them on the first day. But that's the end of it, right, Zack?"

"Sure, dude, we were just fooling around." Zack patted Peter on the back. A small smile appeared on Peter's face as he tried to laugh along with everyone else. Meanwhile, Marty turned to Zack. "Okay, guys, enough funny stuff. Let's get to bed."

We drifted back to our bunks. Peter stayed in the bathroom to rinse the detergent out of the Water Pik. Then he came out. We all watched as he pulled back his blanket and hopped into bed.

Ripppp! Peter's eyes went wide and his jaw dropped. With those long toenails, his feet must've torn right through the sheet!

Creak! Before he had time to react, the bottom of the bed parted where Dan had pulled out the springs.

Thwamp! Peter and his mattress sank through the opening and settled on the floor.

"Hey!" Peter struggled to get out of the bed. The mattress had closed around him like a glove. His arms and legs waved wildly like a beetle who'd been turned upside down. No matter how hard he tried, he couldn't get enough of a grip to lift himself out.

Meanwhile, Dan and Zack were doubled over with laughter. But this time, Marty didn't smile as he helped Peter out of his bed. As soon as Peter was on his feet, he bolted out the screen door and disappeared outside.

Marty glared at us angrily, then followed Peter into the dark.

17

We waited around in the cabin for Marty and Peter to come back. Dan chewed nervously on his fingernails and toyed with his diamond stud earring.

"Maybe we went too far, Zack," he said.

Zack smirked and pushed his fingers through his bushy blond hair. "What can they do? Throw all four of us out of camp on the first day? Forget it. Our parents would all ask for refunds. Old Man Mailer's too tight to give back a cent."

"You think Peter'll come back?" Rick asked.

"I hope not," Zack said. "You really want a geek like that in our cabin?"

Rick and I exchanged another look. I got the feeling he didn't feel any better about what just happened than I did. But if we both felt that way, how come we couldn't stand up to Zack and tell him to lay off Peter?

We waited. The only sound in the cabin was that kid Lewis, lying on the bunk above Peter's, slowly thumbing through a car magazine.

After a while, Marty came back. The corners of his mouth curled down. "Congratulations, guys, you've probably ruined Peter's summer."

"It was just a joke," Zack said with a shrug.

"No, it wasn't just a joke," Marty replied angrily. "It was too many jokes and all aimed at the same kid. After a while it changes from a joke to a message. And Peter heard it loud and clear."

"So where is he?" Rick asked.

"He's staying in another cabin tonight," Marty said. "Right now he's termined to leave camp tomorrow. I'm going to see if I can talk him out of it, but have my doubts." He leveled his gaze at Zack. "Congratulations on a job well ne, jerk."

Zack shrugged. Marty got some things out of Peter's cubby.

"I'm going to bring him his stuff," he said. "It's way past lights out, so just go bed. Last guy turns off the lights."

Marty left the cabin again.

"Man, what a dork," Zack muttered.

"Yeah," Dan agreed.

I washed up and climbed into my bunk. The camp pillow was hard and mpy, and the blanket itched. A few moments later, Rick turned off the lights and alked with his flashlight to the bunk under mine.

I lay in the dark feeling really bad. It looked like I'd managed to get in with e cool guys. But in doing so, I'd helped ruin Peter Peeling's summer. And he'd ne nothing to deserve it. It wasn't his fault that he was dorky, or that he had an erprotective mother.

I yawned and felt myself growing sleepy. My first day of camp was over. it I knew that if I had it to do all over again, I would do it differently.

18

DAY TWO

The bus went over a bump and I felt my eyes open. *Wha ... ? Where was I? On a bus? How?* I sat up straight and looked out the window. The bus was pulling into a big gravel parking lot. Other buses were already there and kids wearing white Camp Walton shirts were climbing out of them.

Wait a minute! I felt a shock race through me. Like being zapped with a cattle prod. It was the same as yesterday. Like, been there, done that! What was going on? Was this a dream? I sure hoped it was.

I looked a few rows ahead and saw the back of Peter Peeling's head. In the row in front of him, Josh and Andy were getting their things together.

I twisted around. In the back seat, Zack, Dan, and Rick were getting up.

It definitely felt more real than a dream.

"Have a nice nap, Sleeping Beauty?" Zack asked with a grin.

Oh no! This was sounding totally too familiar.

"What's the matter?" Zack asked me. "Can't talk?"

"I can talk," I said.

"Good, we were worried there for a moment." Zack smiled as he, Dan, and Rick filed down the aisle past me.

"See ya in the cabin," said Rick.

I watched them go down the aisle. Meanwhile, Peter stood up, clutching his white shopping bag.

"Cool bag," said Zack with a chuckle.

Same as yesterday ...

I was stuck in the first day of camp!

19

Why me?

I took a deep breath and let it out slowly. Well, maybe I shouldn't have been so surprised. The reason I wasn't totally instantly freaked out of my skull was that this wasn't the first time it had happened. Last time I'd gotten stuck in the first day of school.

The difference between last time and this time was simple. Last time I didn't know why I'd been stuck in the same day over and over again. This time it was obvious.

Whoever was in charge of these things decided I was going to do the first day over again.

Because of Peter.

In a strange way I was sort of glad, because this time I'd do it right.

I grabbed my day pack and started down the aisle, but when I got to Peter's seat, I stopped.

"Have a good ride?" I asked him. Meanwhile, in the seat in front of Peter, Andy and Josh swiveled around and watched.

Peter gave me an uncertain look. "Uh, it was okay, I guess."

"I fell asleep," I said. "Was it a long trip?"

"Just a couple of hours," Peter said. "Not too bad."

"Well, come on," I said, hitching my day pack over my shoulder. "We better get off."

"Uh, yeah." If Peter was acting a little wary, it was probably because I'd acted like I didn't want to sit with him before. Of course I couldn't explain why The only thing I could do was be really friendly now.

Peter and I got off the bus, followed by Josh and Andy. Outside, the driver was pulling the duffle bags out of the luggage carrier. Rick, Dan, and Zack were waiting for theirs.

"There's my duffle," Peter said, and went to get it. That's when I felt a tap on my shoulder. Wheeling around, I found Josh and Andy behind me.

"What's with you?" Josh asked in a low voice.

"What are you talking about?" I played dumb.

"When you got on the bus you acted like you didn't want to sit next to that Peeling kid," Andy said. "Now you're acting like best friends. So, what gives?"

"The reason I didn't sit with him was because

I knew I was gonna sleep," I lied. "I mean, forget what he looks like. The guy's in my cabin and I'm gonna be friendly with him no matter what."

Josh and Andy shared a funny look, but didn't say anything more about it. By then Peter had gotten his duffle bag and was headed toward our cabin.

"I guess our cabins will be up that way, too," Josh said.

"No, you guys are over there." I pointed toward the cabins on the other side the athletic field.

Andy frowned. "How do you know that?"

"It's weird," I said with a shrug. "I just feel like I've been here before."

I saw the driver pull out my duffle bag and drop it to the ground with a thud ar where Zack, Dan, and Rick were standing. I went over and struggled to pick it .

Dan started to smile.

"No, it's not bowling balls," I said.

He scowled.

By now, Andy and Josh had gotten their duffle bags and spoke to the guy th the clipboard. Andy turned and looked at me with a puzzled expression. "You re right. Our cabins are over there. How'd you know?"

I was going to explain how I'd seen it all in my crystal ball. But out of the rner of my eye I saw Peter's white shopping bag split and all his stuff spill out to the ground.

The cool guys were going to catch up to him any second. I quickly turned ck to Andy and Josh.

"Gotta run, dudes," I said.

20

Peter put down his duffle and started to pick up his stuff, including the Water Pik.

"Hey, guys, look," Zack was saying as I caught up to them. "A Water Pik."

"Whoa." Dan grinned. "This guy takes serious care of his teeth."

"It's for my gums," Peter tried to explain.

"Gums, huh?" chuckled Dan. "Hey, maybe we should call him Gummi Bear."

"Yeah, and maybe we should call you Gummi Brains," I said.

The cool guys spun around and stared at me. I felt weird. Like in that insta I had just become their enemy.

"Well, look who's here. It's Sleeping Beauty," Zack said. He nudged Dan. "You gonna take that from him?"

Dan narrowed his eyes at me. He was shorter than me, but more powerfull built. I felt my stomach tighten. I didn't want to fight, but I might not have a choice.

"Didn't you say you were in B-13?" Dan asked.

"That's right."

"Better learn to sleep with one eye open," he warned me, then turned to the others. "Come on, guys, let's let these two geeks get to know each other."

Zack and Dan started toward the cabin. Rick gave me a puzzled look, and then followed. I kneeled down with Peter and helped him pick up his stuff.

"Thanks, Jake," he said.

"Hey, always available to help pick stuff up," I said with a grin.

"That's not what I meant," Peter said.

"I know." I winked at him.

Between the two of us, we managed to pick up all his stuff.

"Maybe we'll get lucky and they'll leave us alone," Peter said under his breath as we walked toward the cabin.

"Yeah." I pretended to agree. But knowing Zack, we were going to be anything *but* lucky.

21

We got into the cabin. The cool guys had already staked out the bunks in the back.

Thunk! I dropped my duffle bag next to the first double decker. Standing by his bunk in the back, Zack leveled his gaze at me. I knew what he was going to say.

"It never fails, right?" I said.

Zack blinked as if I'd taken the words out of his mouth.

Peter came in and dropped his duffle bag next to mine. "What never fails?" he asked me in a low voice.

"The jerks take the bunks in the back," I whispered.

Peter grinned.

Just like the day before, Lewis was the last kid in the cabin. This time the only bed left was the top of Rick's double decker.

"Looks like we've got ourselves a real winner cabin this year," Zack muttered.

"Yeah, I wonder if it's too late to get a transfer," Dan replied.

I could have said something, but I decided to keep my mouth shut. There was no sense in asking for trouble. I was pretty sure I was going to have enough of it anyway.

A little later Marty came in and told us all to introduce ourselves. I turned to Peter and told him to come with me.

"Why?" he asked when he saw that I was heading toward the back of the cabin.

"You'll see," I said.

Peter reluctantly followed me. I stopped next to Zack's bunk.

"Listen, Zack," I said. "This is Peter Peeling. And that's what he wants to be called, not Gummi Bear. Our parents were friends when we were little. I haven't seen him in a long time, but he's a good guy."

Zack gave me a blank look. Then a slight smile crept onto his lips. "He can't introduce himself?"

"Well, you guys gave him a pretty hard time before," I said.

"What are you, his bodyguard?" Dan sneered.

"Look, we don't all have to be friends, okay?" I said. "But we do have to live together in this cabin. Now we can either have a good time or a miserable time. It's up to you."

Zack nodded slowly. "Thanks for telling me that, Sleeping Beauty." Then he offered his hand to Peter. "I'm Zack Zanko."

"Uh, hi," Peter replied and shook his hand.

For a split second I felt pretty good. Like maybe things would work out after all. But then Peter's face turned pale and he started to wince. I looked down at their hands. Zack was squeezing so hard his knuckles had turned white.

"Nice to meet you, Peter," Zack said with an icy grin.

22

After Zack let go of Peter's hand, we went back to unpacking. Marty left for

water-front and Zack looked up at Lewis, who was kneeling on his bunk,

king up his car pictures.

"Guess you're into cars, huh?" Zack asked.

Lewis nodded.

"*Small* cars, right?" Zack said.

"*Fast* cars," Lewis replied.

"*Small* fast cars, then," said Zack with a grin.

In the back of the cabin Dan snickered. Hearing it again really made me

d.

"The jerk-magnet says 'What?' " I said in a low voice.

Zack turned and frowned. "What?"

Rick smiled.

"Why do you have to pick on everybody?" I asked Zack.

This time Zack didn't look surprised that I'd interfered. "I wasn't talking to

u, Sleeping Beauty."

"Well, I'm talking to you," I said, facing him.

"Hey," Lewis said from up on his bunk. Zack and I both looked up at him.

wis was looking at me. "Thanks, but I can take care of myself."

"Whoa!" Dan chuckled. "Sounds like we got a whole cabin full of tough guys."

"Yeah." Zack cracked his knuckles. "Maybe it's time to find out just how tough everyone really is."

"Hey, who wants to play that new tetherball game?" Rick suddenly asked.

Zack looked around. "Yeah, sure, let's play." He turned to Peter. "Wanna play some tetherball, Gummi Bear?"

"Uh, I'm not sure," Peter replied nervously.

Zack put his hands on his hips. "What are you, some kind of wuss?"

"No, he's not a wuss," I said. "Not only that, but he'll play you on one foot and with one hand behind his back."

"I will?" Peter asked, bewildered.

Zack scowled, then grinned. "That's just what I was gonna say. Okay, let's do it!"

He, Dan, and Rick went outside. Peter hesitated and looked at me. "What's tetherball?"

"It's the game with the pole and the ball on the rope," I said. "Don't worry, you can do it."

Peter's eyes darted around nervously. "But I haven't finished unpacking. Marty said we had to finish unpacking before we — " "Yeah, I know," I said. "B if you don't go out there and play, Zack is going to give you grief forever. You can finish unpacking later."

Peter winced at the thought of facing Zack in tetherball.

"Go on, Peter," I urged him. "You don't have to beat him, just go out there and show that you're willing to play."

"Aren't you coming?" Peter asked.

"Sure," I said. "I'll be out in a second."

"Promise?" Peter asked.

"Yeah, honest, I promise."

Peter went out the screen door. I looked up at Lewis, who was still tacking car pictures to the rafters.

"Hey, Lewis?" I said.

"Yeah." He paused and looked down at me.

"About what happened before," I said. "The only reason I spoke up against Zack is because I think you, me, and Peter better stick together, okay?"

"Why?" Lewis asked.

"Because I have a feeling those guys are gonna cause a lot of trouble for us," I said.

Lewis gazed past me. It seemed like he was looking out the screen door at the cool guys, who were getting ready to play tetherball. "Thanks, Jake. But like I said before, I can take care of myself."

I left the cabin. Zack, Dan, and Rick were standing by the tetherball court with Peter. Zack was already on one foot, waiting while Peter tried to decide which foot and hand to use. The poor guy was totally uncoordinated. Zack was going to demolish him.

"Hey, wait a minute," I said. "This isn't really fair."

Zack rolled his eyes. "Now what?"

"Well, tetherball is something you're really good at," I said. "So of course you're gonna beat Peter. If he has to play you in tetherball, then you should agree to play him at something he's really good at."

"Okay, sure," Zack said with a sigh. "What'll it be, Gummi Bear?"

"Uh ..." Peter had to think. "How about Scrabble?"

"Scrabble?" Zack repeated in disbelief. Dan clamped his hand over his mouth to keep from laughing out loud. Even I had to admit it wasn't the best idea.

"Isn't there something else?" I asked Peter. "You know, something you guys can play outsider

Peter bit his lip. "Croquet?"

"You mean, with the wooden balls and the mallets and the wire thingies?" Dan asked.

"They're called wickets," Peter informed him.

"Oh, man." Zack shook his head and groaned. "What a dork!"

Peter gave me a pleading look, like he hoped I'd come to his rescue. I really wanted to, but it wasn't going to be easy.

23

Fortunately, before Zack had a chance to slaughter Peter in one-handed tetherball, Marty arrived and took us to lunch. The cool guys went ahead and Peter and I followed.

"Just my luck," Peter muttered under his breath.

"What do you mean?" I asked.

"I have to get stuck in a cabin with those guys," he said.

"I have a feeling there might be guys like that in any cabin," I said.

Peter nodded. "Well, then I guess I'm lucky that we're in this together."

Maybe, I thought.

Once again the dining hall was noisy and crowded with kids. I saw Josh and Andy.

"Catch you later," I said to Peter, planning to go talk to my friends.

"Where're you going?" he asked.

"Uh, just to talk to my friends," I said.

Peter glanced at the table where B-13 sat. The cool guys were already there. He turned to me. "Uh, can I come with you?"

"Hey, don't worry," I said. "I'll be back in a minute."

Peter didn't look happy, but he headed toward the table while I headed toward my friends.

"How's it going with the cool guys and Peter the dork?" Andy asked.

"They're really giving him grief," I said.

"You standing up for him?" Andy asked.

"Better believe it."

Andy and Josh traded an uncertain look.

"You sure that's what you want to do?" Josh asked.

"Hey, someone's got to do it," I said. "Otherwise, the kid's gonna be this mmer's sacrificial lamb."

"Yeah, but how about *you?*" Andy asked.

"What about me?" I asked, not understanding what he meant.

"How are you gonna have any fun if you're always defending Peter?" he ed.

Out of the corner of my eye, I saw Mr. Mailer, the owner of the camp, lking toward the microphone. I knew I wouldn't have time to explain to my ends that I was trapped in the first day of camp, and that I was pretty certain that only way I could get out of it was by defending Peter.

"Hey, look, guys," I said. "I'm just trying to do the right thing."

Josh was just about to say something when Mr. Mailer got on the crophone and started his speech about how glad he was that we were all there, w much fun we'd have, and what a big happy family we'd be. I said good-bye to my friends, and went back to our table. I sat next to Peter, who had twisted arou

in his seat to listen to Mr. Mailer. Zack and Dan were giving each other looks.

Little did they know that I knew what they were planning.

24

Mr. Mailer's speech ended, and everyone turned back to the table. The camp waiters were coming out of the kitchen with the trays of American Chop Suey. Zack started to reach for the metal pitcher in the middle of the table, but I grabbed it first and stood up. "Who wants bug juice?"

"Me," Peter said.

I looked down at his glass. It was covered with the plastic wrap. "Oh, gee, your glass has something on it."

Peter stared down at his glass, then removed the plastic wrap. I poured the bright red bug juice.

"Anyone else?" I asked, turning toward the cool guys.

Zack was sitting with his arms crossed, glowering at me. He was obviously mad that I'd foiled his trick.

"I'll have some." Dan held up his glass.

With the pitcher in my hand, I stretched across the table toward him. Unfortunately, I missed! Bright red bug juice splashed all over the table in front of Dan and onto his shirt.

"Hey! What're you doing!" Dan yelled and jumped up.

"Oh, gee, I'm really sorry," I pretended to gasp.

Meanwhile, Zack started to laugh ... until I "accidentally" spilled bug juice on him too.

"You idiot!" Zack shouted and jumped up. His shirt had a big red stain on it.

"Sorry," I apologized.

"No, you're not!" Zack growled, making a fist. "You did it on purpose!"

The next thing I knew, he started around the table toward me with both hands balled into fists. Luckily for me, Marty got up and blocked his path.

"Chill out, Zack," our counselor said. "Jake said it was an accident."

"Bull," Zack sputtered. "He knew exactly what he was doing. He did it because of the plastic wrap on Gummi Bear's glass. He — "

"That reminds me," Marty said. "Just how did the plastic wrap get on Peter's glass?"

Zack suddenly quieted down. He glared past Marty at me. "You're dead meat, Sleeping Beauty."

"Ooh, I'm really scared," I replied.

"Both of you, knock it off," Marty ordered.

"Zack and Dan, go back to the cabin and put on dry clothes. Jake, you promise to be more careful pouring the bug juice next time?"

"You bet." I nodded.

Zack and Dan left. The waiters served lunch and once again we stared at the American Chop Suey in disbelief. I figured the bug juice incident was behind us, so I was surprised when Marty looked up from his plate and said, "Hey, Jake, did you do it on purpose?"

"Uh ..." I didn't know what to say.

"Tell the truth," our counselor said.

"Okay, yeah, I did," I answered.

"Why?" Marty asked.

"Because I don't like the way they pick on Peter," I said.

Marty nodded as if he understood. "No more of that."

25

After lunch, Marty gave us the tour of the camp and then told us we had free time until dinner. I suggested to Peter that we do something together.

"Like what?" he asked.

"I don't know," I said as I watched Rick, Zack, and Dan head for the basketball court. "What do you want to do?"

"Well..." Peter scratched his head. "You want to play Scrabble?"

Playing Scrabble was close to the last thing in the world I wanted to do. "Hey, look," I said. "It's a beautiful day. Why don't we do something outside?"

"We could play Scrabble outside," Peter said.

I couldn't help but sigh. I had made it my sworn duty to protect Peter from the cool guys, and make sure he had a decent time at camp. It was the right thing to do. Besides, if I didn't I'd probably be trapped in the first day of camp forever. And if I had to look at American Chop Suey one more time, I was going to barf.

But it wasn't going to be easy to help Peter. The absolute last thing I wanted to do was play Scrabble *outside*. If anyone saw us we'd be labeled super-mega-*quadra*-dorks.

"I really think we should save Scrabble for a rainy day," I said. "Isn't there anything else you'd like to do?"

"Uh . . ." Peter rubbed his chin. "That nature walk sounds pretty interesting."

The nature walk!? Inwardly I groaned. But at least we'd be outside. Besides,

robably wouldn't have to worry about running into anyone I knew. The only

ys we'd meet on the nature walk were bound to be dorks.

26

""What happened to you?" Josh asked when I saw him and Andy outside t
dining hall before dinner that night.

"Peter wanted to go on a nature walk," I said, scratching my arm.

"A nature walk?" Andy made a face.

"Hey, it was an educational experience," I said, scratching my ear. "I learn
about three different kinds of butterflies, two different kinds of skunk cabbage, a
painted turtle, and a red-winged bluebird."

"Blackbird" Josh corrected me.

"Whatever," I said with a shrug.

Andy studied my face. "I count seven mosquito bites on the left side of yo
forehead alone."

"The grand body total's somewhere around sixty," I said, scratching my
neck. My head, neck, and arms were covered with itching red welts. The nature
walk had led Peter and me through a mosquito-infested swamp.

Josh shook his head. "Look, I know you're trying to be a nice guy, Jake. B
maybe you ought to spend a little less time with Peter. Not just because everyone
going to think of you as a dork by association, but it's also hazardous to your
health."

"I can't," I said.

"Why not?"

I looked around to make sure no one else was listening. Then in a low voice I said, "Because I'm trapped in the first day of camp."

"You're *what?*" Josh's forehead wrinkled.

"I'm trapped in the first day of camp," I said. "Today's the first day of camp for you, but for me, yesterday was."

"Yesterday we were back in Jeffersonville," Andy said. "We went Rollerblading, remember?"

"You did," I said. "I was here at camp."

"No, you weren't," Josh said. "You were with us."

I shook my head. "Listen, I know this is really hard to explain, but this is the second time I've been through this day. Yesterday when we got to camp I tried to be one of the cool guys. I picked on Peter. That was the wrong thing to do so I got punished. They're making me do the day over again."

"Who's making you do it over?" Andy asked.

"I don't know who," I said. "But it's happened to me before. Remember the first day of school last year when Alex Silver decided to be the Knight of Wedgy and wedgy everyone?"

"Oh, yeah." Andy grinned at the memory. "He thought he was so totally cool."

"Well, originally I was into it too," I said. "We were the Knights of Wedgy together. I mean, you have to admit that it feels good to be in with the cool guys."

Andy and Josh both nodded.

"But the thing is," I went on. "If you have to pick on kids to prove you're cool, are you really cool? Or are you just some jerk who has to scare kids into thinking he's cool?"

Josh made a funny face. "What does this have to do with going through the first day of camp over again?"

"I had to do the first day of school over about six times before I figured out that being nice to people is better than being mean and cool," I explained. "So now that I'm stuck in the first day of camp I know I have to be really nice to Peter and protect him from the cool guys. Once I've done that, I'll be able to get to the second day of camp."

Josh and Andy shared another doubtful glance.

Then Josh cleared his throat. "I hate to say this, Jake, but are you aware of the fact that you've totally wigged out?"

"Look, it's dumb to argue about this," I said. "You'll never believe me. I probably shouldn't have told you. The weird thing is that it doesn't actually matter. After today everything's going to be normal anyway."

"Except that you and Peter the Geek are joined at the hip," Andy pointed

out.

"If Jake really believes this stuff about being trapped in the first day of

camp, maybe he should be joined with Peter at the hip," Josh said.

"You mean, like two peas in a pod?" Andy asked.

"More like two nuts in a shell," Josh said.

I just smiled. "Whatever you say, guys."

27

After dinner was the movie. I sat on the bench in the back of the dining hall with Peter and the other guys from our cabin. As soon as the movie started, Marty warned us not to get into any trouble, and left. Then the cool guys left.

"Where're they going?" Peter whispered to me.

"Back to the cabin," I whispered back.

"Why?"

"To set booby traps for us."

In the dark, Peter frowned. "How do you know?"

"Trust me," I said in a low voice. "Now listen, I'm gonna leave too. If I don't get back here before the movie ends, tell Marty I had a bad stomachache and went to the nurse."

"Where are you really going?" Peter whispered back.

"I'm going to take care of a few things," I said and started to slide down the bench. Then I stopped and turned back to Peter.

"One last thing," I said. "After the movie you're gonna go get ice cream and Zack's gonna start acting really friendly to you."

"Why?" Peter asked.

"Because he wants to set you up," I explained. "He wants you to think he's ng to be your pal so that you won't expect the booby traps. Anyway, when he s it, act like you think he's sincere."

"Why?" Peter asked.

"Because that's how we'll set him up," I replied with a wink.

I left the dining hall. Outside the crickets were chirping in the moonlight. Up ad I could see Zack and his buddies walking quickly back to the cabin. That's ere I was headed too, but instead of following them, I snuck around the back of cabins until I got to B-13.

Standing on my tiptoes behind the cabin I was able to peek in through the eened bathroom window. The cabin was dark and I couldn't see much, but I ld hear whispers and the squeak of bedsprings as the cool guys set their traps.

Little did they know that I had a few booby traps of my own to set.

Leaving the back of the cabin, I snuck around the side and found the hose. I ught it around to the front of the cabin and left the nozzle next to the big patch dirt at the bottom of the front steps. I let the water run slowly and quietly, ating a big mud puddle.

Next I borrowed the clothesline and tied it across the bottom step to the ch, about eight inches from the floor. In the dark, the cool guys would never see

Now it was time to sit back and wait.

About fifteen minutes later, the front door of the cabin creaked open and Zack came out, followed by Dan and Rick. Crouching around the side of the cab I peeked up and watched.

"Okay, dudes," Zack said as he crossed the porch and started down the fro steps. "Let's get back to the ... *Ahhh!*"

He tripped over the clothesline.

Ker-splat!

Zack fell face-first into the mud puddle.

Up on the porch, Dan looked shocked. Rick had a slight grin on his face. I was starting to wonder whose side that guy was really on.

"What the ... ?" Zack jumped to his feet in the middle of the puddle. The whole front half of his body was soaked brown with mud. It was in his hair and c his face. His arms and legs were covered.

"Hey, check this out." Dan pointed at the clothesline tied across the bottor step. "Looks like someone booby trapped us while we were booby trapping Gummi Bear."

Zack looked around, fuming. "I bet I know who it was, too."

"So what are you gonna do?" Dan asked.

"I'm gonna take a shower and change my clothes," Zack said. "Then I'm gonna find Sleeping Beauty and destroy him."

28

Rick and Dan headed back to the dining hall.

Zack went back into the cabin to change his clothes and clean up. As soon as I heard the shower start to run, I snuck in. The cabin was dark. Only the bathroom light was on. Picking my way around the bunks, I quietly found the pen light in Zack's cubby. Holding the light between my teeth, I pulled every pair of pants and shorts out of his cubby. Then I snuck back out and hid them under the porch.

A couple of minutes later the shower stopped. Zack muttered angrily to himself as he toweled off. He kept grumbling about how he was going to break my skull and make me eat mud. He left the bathroom and headed back to his bunk to put on clean clothes.

"Huh? What the???"

He'd just discovered that he had no pants or shorts. "Oh, man, I'll kill that kid," he muttered. "Just wait till I find him. I'm gonna break both of his arms."

A few moments later the door of the cabin swung open and slammed closed. From around the corner of the cabin I watched Zack head back toward the dining hall wearing a pair of Dan's shorts all bunched up at the waist.

There was still work to do. Luckily, I had time because the guys were going to go for ice cream after the movie.

I went back into the cabin and found the springs Dan had taken from Peter's and my double-decker bunk. After putting them back where they belonged, I unshort-sheeted our beds and rinsed the detergent out of Peter's Water Pik.

Now it was time to get to work on Zack and Dan's bunk.

29

I was lying on my bed when the cabin door creaked open and Marty came in, followed by the rest of the guys.

"What happened to you?" Marty asked.

"I had a stomachache and went to see the nurse," I said. "I just got back here a few minutes ago."

"Does it still hurt?" he asked.

"Naw, it's a lot better," I said.

Marty told the rest of the guys to get ready for bed. When Zack passed my bunk, he squinted angrily to let me know that I hadn't fooled him. I smiled back.

Just like the night before, the cool guys stalled and pretended to be busy so that Peter would be the first to use the bathroom. Finally, Peter got his Water Pik and went into the bathroom humming to himself. I'd warned him about what was going to happen, so he knew he had to pretend to be in a good mood and act like he thought the cool guys liked him.

As soon as Peter went into the bathroom, Zack quickly motioned for the cool guys to follow. They huddled outside the doorway and listened. The Water Pik started to whir. Peter was still humming to himself. The humming and whirring mixed together as he started to clean his teeth.

And that's the way it stayed until Peter finished.

Frowning, Zack turned away from the bathroom entrance. Once again, he

ked up at me on my bunk and narrowed his eyes. He must've realized that I'd

done his booby traps.

The rest of the guys brushed their teeth and washed up. Then Zack climbed

to his bunk. At the same time, Dan pulled back his blanket and started to get in

bed below.

Sploosh!

Rip!

Zack's mouth fell open. I'd not only short-sheeted his and Dan's beds, I'd

led a few water balloons for good measure. He'd not only torn through his

ets, but soaked his mattress as well.

Zack stared daggers at me. "Why you!"

He jumped out of bed, but Marty stepped into his path.

"What's the matter, Zack?" our counselor asked with a smile. "Can't take a

e?"

Zack was seething, balling and unballing his fists, his face red with fury. He

glared past Marty at me and didn't reply.

Dan and Zack went to get new sheets. While they were out Marty talked to

"Listen, Jake," he said, barely able to hide his smile. "Let's not have any more of that kind of stuff, okay?"

I nodded, but really got the feeling our counselor was glad that Zack had gotten what he deserved. Peter winked at me and smiled. Lewis looked sort of amused. Rick listened and watched, but said nothing. Still, he didn't look annoyed or anything.

Zack and Dan came back with some towels and dry sheets. They spread the towels over the wet spots on their mattresses, then made their beds with the new sheets and got in.

"Oh, man," Dan moaned. "The water still seeps through."

Zack didn't say anything, but I imagined the water had seeped through his sheets, too.

Marty turned off the cabin lights and told us to go to sleep. I lay in bed in the dark. Despite that hard, lumpy pillow and itchy blanket, I felt pretty good. I'd done the right thing this time. Hopefully with my help, Peter would have a half-decent summer.

And I would get out of being trapped in the first day of camp.

I was just falling asleep when I heard the faintest whisper come from the direction of Zack's bunk. "Hey, Sleeping Beauty."

"What?" I whispered back.

"You better get a good night's rest," Zack whispered. "Because tomorrow you're dead meat."

I rolled over and pulled my pillow over my head so I wouldn't have to listen to any more of his threats.

But it made me wonder.

Maybe I'd made things better for Peter. But I'd also made them pretty bad for me.

Was that the way it had to be?

DAY THREE

I felt a bump and opened my eyes. *Huh? What was I doing on the bus?*

It must have been a dream.

I closed my eyes.

Then opened them again.

I was still on the bus.

And it didn't feel like a dream.

This was weird.

Because it *had* to be a dream.

I sat up and looked out the window. We were pulling into the parking lot. The other buses were already there and the new campers wearing white Camp Walton T-shirts were climbing out. Next I looked inside the bus. Peter was in his seat a few rows ahead. In the row in front of him, Josh was taking off his headphones, and Andy was closing his magazine.

I twisted around. In the backseat, Zack, Dan, and Rick were getting up.

"Have a nice nap, Sleeping Beauty?" Zack asked with a grin.

Uh-oh!

This was no dream!

It was happening again! But why? How was it possible? *I'd done the right thing the day before!*

"What's the matter?" Zack asked. "Can't talk?"

"Uh ..." I didn't know what to say. I didn't know what to do. I was trapped in the first day of camp again. But it didn't make sense. Hadn't I done what I was supposed to do to get out of this mess?

Why hadn't it worked?

Zack raised an eyebrow. "Is 'uh' all you can say?"

He was waiting for me to say something, but I didn't know what to do. If being friendly didn't work, and being *unfriendly* was no good either, then what was the answer?

I looked up into Zack's face as he, Dan, and Rick filed down the aisle past me. Zack's mouth was a hard, straight line. Dan gave me a curious look.

I stretched and yawned.

"See ya in the cabin," said Rick.

They passed Peter as he stood up with his white paper shopping bag. Zack made his comment about the bag, and Dan chuckled. Once again, Peter looked away and waited until they left the bus. Then he went down the aisle and got off.

And that left Josh, Andy, and me on the bus. I knew Josh would ask why I didn't sit with them, and Andy would accuse me of not wanting to sit with Peter because I wanted to make friends with the cool guys.

"You're right," I said before either of them had a chance to speak. "I didn't feel like sitting with Peter. But I didn't make friends with the cool guys either. And I don't think I'm going to."

Josh blinked with surprise. "How'd you know I was gonna ask about that?"

"Because that's what you asked me yesterday," I said.

"What are you talking about?" he said. "How could I have asked that yesterday?"

"Because we were all on this bus and you asked me why I didn't want to sit with you," I explained.

Andy and Josh shared a bewildered look.

"I've got news for you, Jake," Andy said. "You weren't here yesterday. Today's the first day of camp."

"It is for you guys," I said. "But it's the third day for me. Actually, it's my first day for the third time."

Josh and Andy traded really worried looks.

"Are you feeling okay?" Josh asked me.

"No, I'm totally freaked," I said. "This is the third time I've stood on this bus talked to you like this. And for all I know I may be doing it for the rest of my

."

"Maybe you need to get some more sleep," Andy said, a little nervously.

"No, guys, I'm telling you the truth," I said. Then I explained how I was ped in the first day of camp, just like I'd once been trapped in the first day of ool.

Neither of my friends said a word when I was done. I could tell from their ressions that they thought I was completely insane.

"Listen, guys, I really need you to believe me," I said desperately. "When I stuck in the first day of school I got out of it by doing the right thing. But I did right thing yesterday and I'm still trapped."

"I think the right thing for you would be to spend the summer in a mental titution," Josh said.

"I'm not joking, guys," I said.

"Uh, boys?" Down at the front of the bus Mr. Mailer had climbed back on. me to get off and get your bags."

"We're coming, Mr. Mailer," I said.

The camp owner got off the bus.

"Who's he?" Andy asked.

"He owns the camp," I said.

"How do you know?" Josh asked.

"I told you. I've been here for three days."

Josh rolled his eyes in disbelief.

"Uh, I think we better get off," Andy said.

We started down the aisle toward the front of the bus.

"Guys," I whispered. "For the last time, you have to help me. I don't know what to do."

"It's simple, Jake," Josh whispered back. "You get off the bus. You were here yesterday. You were back in Jeffersonville. We spent the day Rollerblading remember?"

"You guys did," I said. "Not me. I spent the day protecting Peter from the cool guys."

"Sure, Jake, whatever you say," Andy whispered.

31

We got off the bus. The driver was pulling the duffle bags out of the luggage carrier. Rick, Dan, and Zack were waiting for theirs. Peter got his duffle bag and headed toward our cabin.

Josh started to say something.

"Your cabins are over there." I pointed toward the cabins on the other side of the athletic field.

"How do you know?" Andy asked.

"I told you," I said wearily. "I've already been here, done this."

"We better check with a counselor just to make sure," Josh said, clearly not trusting me.

"Thanks for believing me, guys," I grumbled bitterly.

Josh had a pained expression on his face. "How are we supposed to believe that you were here yesterday when we were with you back in Jeffersonville?"

I was tired of trying to explain it. Maybe I was expecting too much from my friends. I mean, even I found it hard to believe. And I was living it!

I left Josh and Andy, and went to get my duffle bag. Dan started to smile. I knew what he was going to ask, of course.

"Grenades, land mines, and mortar shells," I said. "I'm a very violent person."

He scowled.

Andy and Josh got their duffle bags and spoke to the guy-with the clipboard, who pointed toward their cabins on the other side of the athletic field.

Andy gave me a puzzled look.

"Believe me now?" I asked.

He didn't answer.

"Want some advice?" I asked.

Josh and Andy nodded.

"Save your snacks. You're gonna hate lunch."

32

I started toward my cabin. Up ahead I saw Peter's white shopping bag split and all his stuff spill out onto the ground. The cool guys were right behind him. My first inclination was to hurry up and help him. But on second thought I decided not to. Before I could help Peter, I had to concentrate on figuring out how to help myself get out of the mess I was in.

Just as on the previous days, the cool guys started to hassle Peter about his Water Pik. I went around them and continued lugging my duffle bag toward the cabin. But it wasn't long before the cool guys, with their lighter bags, passed me.

This time I got to the cabin about the same time as Lewis. Inside, the cool guys had already staked out the back two bunks. Lewis and I put down our duffle bags and glanced at each other. I pointed at the bunk closest to the front of the cabin.

"Want to share this one?" I asked.

Lewis nodded.

"Top or bottom?" I asked.

"I'll take the top," he said.

"You don't want to take that one, Sleeping Beauty," Zack said from his bunk in the back of the cabin. "Only the dweebs want to be close to the counselor."

"Come on back here with us," said Rick. "You can take the top of my bunk."

"No, thanks," I said, and started to unpack.

Peter was the last camper to enter the cabin. The only bed left was the top of Rick's double decker. Peter lugged his stuff toward it.

Zack turned to Rick. "Must be your lucky day," he said with a snigger.

Lewis and I glanced at each other, but said nothing.

Once again it took a while to get all my stuff unpacked. I knew I had to do something different if I wanted to get out of the first day of camp, but I still didn't know what to do. Then Marty arrived and showed us how the cabin worked. After he left for the waterfront, Zack strolled toward my bunk. Lewis was on top, tacking up his car pictures. Zack went through the small, fast car routine. Lewis told him to get lost, thereby earning the nickname of Mighty Mouse.

"So we got Mighty Mouse and Sleeping Beauty in the first bunk," Zack said, taunting us. Lewis stuck another picture on the rafter and didn't say a word.

Zack turned to me. "Wanna play some tetherball, Sleeping Beauty?"

"No, thanks," I replied.

"What's wrong?" Zack said. "You chicken, Sleeping Beauty? Maybe we'll have to call you Sleeping Chicken."

"Or Chicken Beauty," added Dan.

"The mucous brain says, 'What?' " I said.

"What?" said Zack.

I caught Rick's eye. He smiled.

Zack put his hands on his hips. "Man, what a winner cabin we've got this

r. Mighty Mouse, Sleeping Chicken, and Gummi Bear."

Following Lewis's lead, I ignored him. Zack turned to Peter and challenged

to play tetherball. When Peter admitted he didn't know what tetherball was,

k and Dan made fun of him. A few moments later, Peter, Dan, and Zack went

side to play. This time Rick followed, then stopped by the screen door until the

ers had gone outside. I was surprised to see him turn to Lewis and me.

"You guys coming?" he asked.

Lewis and I both shook our heads. Rick paused for a moment as if he wasn't

tain what to do. Then he went outside.

As soon as Rick had gone, Lewis went to the screen door and looked out.

could hear Zack and Dan laughing as Zack humiliated Peter in tetherball.

ide, Lewis just watched.

Meanwhile, I kept wondering how I was ever going to get out of the first day

amp.

33

Later we all went to the dining hall for lunch. I walked alone, a dozen yards behind Zack, Rick, and Dan. Behind me Lewis and Peter talked quietly.

Just as on the first day, I wondered what they were talking about. This time slowed my pace and tried to eavesdrop.

"You have to stand up to them," Lewis was saying. "If you don't, they're going to make you miserable the whole time you're here."

I slowed up even more. Now I was walking with them. Peter gave me a nervous look out of the corner of his eye.

"There's one thing I don't get," I said quietly to Lewis. "When you stood up to Zack before, how'd you know he wouldn't just haul back and smash you?"

"I didn't know for sure," Lewis said. "But I figured he'd have to be really stupid to do something like that on the first day of camp. Besides, I think he's mostly talk."

Peter just listened, but didn't say anything.

Once again, Josh, Andy, and I met before lunch.

"Still think you're trapped in the first day of camp?" Josh asked.

"I don't think it," I said. "I knew it."

Josh and Andy shared an uncomfortable look.

"So how's it going with the cool guys and Peter the dweeb?" Andy asked.

"They're really giving him grief," I said.

"You standing up for him?" Andy asked.

"That doesn't work," I said.

Andy and Josh gave each other another funny look.

"What do you mean?" asked Andy.

"I mean I tried it yesterday and it didn't work," I said.

"You tried what yesterday?" Josh asked.

"I protected Peter from the cool guys," I said.

"Jake, I'm really getting worried about you," Andy said. "We keep telling you that you weren't here yesterday."

"And I keep telling you I was," I said. "You think I want to spend the rest of my life trapped in the first day of camp, eating American Chop Suey for lunch every day?"

Josh wrinkled his nose. "What's American Chop Suey?"

"You'll know in about a minute," I said.

Both Josh and Andy were quiet for a moment. Then Josh said, "Okay, Jake, for the sake of argument, let's say you really are stuck in the first day of camp. What are Andy and I supposed to do about it?"

That was a good question.

"I don't know," I said. "But it definitely feels better knowing that someone believes me."

By now, Mr. Mailer was standing at the microphone. He began his speech welcoming us to camp.

"Guess we better get back to our tables," Josh said.

"See you later, Jake." Andy said.

"One last thing," I said. "Whatever you do this afternoon, don't go on the nature walk."

Josh and Andy gave me bewildered looks. Then shaking their heads in puzzlement, they went back to their tables.

34

By the time I got back to my table, Peter was twisted around in his seat, listening to Mr. Mailer's welcoming speech. Dan was reaching across the table and putting the plastic wrap over Peter's glass.

I locked eyes with Lewis, and we shared a knowing look. But then he looked away. I just didn't get it. If protecting Peter wasn't the right thing to do, then what was? Certainly not joining the cool guys and picking on him. What other choice was there?

Mr. Mailer's speech ended. The camp waiters were coming out of the kitchen with big trays of American Chop Suey. Meanwhile, Zack reached for the metal pitcher in the middle of the table. "Who wants bug juice?"

"Me, me, me, me." Everyone at the table said they wanted some.

"Here you go." Zack stood up and poured out the bug juice. Just as he had on the first day, he held the pitcher high so that a long red stream cascaded into the glass in front of each kid.

Finally every glass except Peter's was filled.

"So, Gummi Bear, you sure you want some?" Zack asked.

Peter nodded.

I just couldn't stand the idea of him getting splattered with bug juice again. Maybe stopping Zack wasn't the right thing to do, but I had to do it anyway.

"Hey, Peter," I said. "Look at your glass."

Peter looked down at his glass. His eyes widened.

"Bombs away." Zack poured.

Peter pulled his glass away and slid his chair back to avoid getting splattered.

Splash! The red bug juice hit the table and splattered in every direction. A little of it landed on Peter, but this time more hit Marty.

"Hey!" Marty jumped up, glowering at Zack. "What'd you do that for?"

"It's not my fault Gummi Bear pulled his glass away," Zack said.

"Yeah, but look." Peter shoved the plastic-covered glass to Marty, who'd grabbed a handful of napkins and started to blot the bug juice off his shirt.

"Who put the plastic on Peter's glass?" Marty asked, looking at Zack and Dan. Neither of them answered. Marty nodded knowingly just the same.

Zack put down the pitcher and sat down looking pretty ticked.

"The bonehead says, 'What?' " I mumbled.

"What?" said Zack.

I winked at Lewis, but he just looked back at me with a blank expression.

The only person who smiled was Rick.

35

After lunch the cool guys went off to play basketball. Peter asked me if I
ıted to go on the nature walk with him. I said I appreciated his asking, but I
ɔn't up to it.

This time I went down to the waterfront. When I got there, Lewis was
ıding on a dock lined with small blue sailboats. He was talking to an older guy
ıring a gray counselor's T-shirt. When Lewis saw me, he waved. "Hey, Jake, got
:cond?"

I went over. "What's up?"

"I was thinking about taking a boat out, but they have a rule that you have to
with a buddy," Lewis said. "Want to go?"

"I don't know how to sail," I said.

"No sweat," said Lewis. "I'll do everything."

A few minutes later I was sitting in the bow of a sailboat. Lewis was in the
n, steering with the rudder and pulling the ropes attached to the white sail
rhead.

The breeze on the lake moved us along at an even pace. Not exactly
lling, but it was relaxing.

"Thanks for coming," Lewis said.

"No prob," I said. "So you like sailing, huh?"

"Naw, I hate it." Lewis smiled a little to let me know he was kidding.

I reached over the side and dipped my hand in the lake. "Brrr, the water's cold."

"Better get used to it," Lewis said.

"Why?"

"Because first thing every morning Marty's gonna make us swim."

"First thing in the morning!?" I gasped. "Are you serious?"

Lewis nodded. "Marty's a swim instructor. I know a guy who was in his cabin last year. He said Marty always makes his cabin do it."

"Bummer," I said.

Lewis agreed. Then we talked about where Lewis learned to sail, and about the sailboat his parents shared with another family. It was sort of strange — how friendly and talkative he was on the sailboat when he was so quiet everywhere el

"As long as I get to sail, this is gonna be a good summer," he said.

"Too bad it won't be good for Peter," I said. "Not with those dipwads pick on him all the time."

"I told him he has to stand up to them," Lewis said.

"Yeah, I know," I said. "But I'm starting to think maybe he doesn't know how."

"Maybe it doesn't matter," Lewis said with a shrug. "Maybe Zack and his friends will get bored picking on Peter and find other things to do."

From the previous days I knew that wouldn't happen. "Er, I doubt it. I think they're planning to mess him up pretty good tonight."

Lewis nodded, but didn't answer.

We sailed around the lake for a while more. There wasn't much for me to do, so I just thought about stuff.

And that's when I had the idea for helping Peter.

It was risky, but it just might work.

36

Once again, everybody met at the cabin before dinner. Even though I hadn't played basketball that afternoon, I still decided to take a shower. When I came out of the bathroom, Zack was bugging Peter about the nature walk again.

"What are you, some kind of freak?" Zack asked.

Peter bowed his head.

"Hey, Zack ..." Rick started to say.

"Yeah, what?" Zack snapped.

"Maybe you should leave the guy alone," Rick said.

"Guy?" Zack smirked and stared straight at Peter. "I don't see a guy. I don't know what I see. It's like something from another planet."

Rick didn't answer. He just looked at me.

"The fleabrain says, 'What?' " I muttered.

"What?" said Zack.

Rick grinned.

"Shower's free," I said.

Zack went into the bathroom. Rick and I both watched him. Then we turned and looked at each other. Whose side was he really on? I wondered.

"What happened to you guys?" I asked Josh and Andy outside the dining hall before dinner that night. They were both covered with red welts.

"We went on the nature walk," Andy said, scratching a bunch of swollen umps on his neck.

"Are you serious?" I gasped. "That's exactly what I told you not to do."

"Yeah, but we had to find out why you didn't want us to do it," Josh said, scratching his arm.

"Because you'd get eaten alive by mosquitos," I said.

"We found that out," said Andy as he scratched his ear.

"So, you still think you're trapped in the first day of camp?" Josh asked.

"I don't think it," I said. "I know it."

Josh and Andy gave each other a skeptical look. Then Josh said, "Okay, isten, we had a talk. We still find this really hard to believe, Jake. But then, we never would have believed that you could get stuck in the President's body, or that Andy would switch bodies with your dog. So just in case it's true, is there anything we can do to help?"

"You guys still have your Cheese Whiz?" I asked.

After dinner we went back to the cabin. Zack and Dan talked in low voices as they planned what they were going to do to Peter later. Then Dan went into the bathroom and stayed forever. After a while, Marty got impatient and called into the bathroom to ask Dan if he was okay, and Dan called back that he'd be out in a econd. Then Zack made the joke about being lost and everyone laughed.

Meanwhile, I turned to Lewis and Peter. "Why don't we wait outside?" I suggested.

As soon as Peter and Lewis came outside, I told them what the cool guys were planning to do to Peter.

"They can't sneak out during the movie," Peter said. "Marty won't let them."

"Marty won't be there to stop them," I said.

Lewis frowned. "How do you know?"

"Uh ..." I couldn't tell him the truth. "I heard some other counselors talking. They said they were going to get together during the movie and try to figure out how to meet the counselors from the girls' camp. I have to believe Marty will be interested."

Lewis gave me a sly grin. "Yeah, well, you're probably right about that."

"If you know what Zack's planning," Peter said, "why don't you tell Marty. Then he'll talk to them."

"Talking to them won't change anything," I said.

Peter gave Lewis a questioning look.

"He's probably right," Lewis said.

Then I told them my plan. Well, not all of it. But most of it.

"I don't know, Jake." Peter swallowed nervously when I'd finished. "If it doesn't work, they could make us really miserable for the next month."

"I'm willing to take that risk," I said. "And if you don't try it, your life is
na be miserable for the next month anyway. Why not give it a shot? At least
way there's a chance things could turn out okay."

Peter's shoulders sagged and he stared at the ground. "Maybe I should just
home. I didn't want to come to camp in the first place."

"You can't just quit," I said. "You can't run away your whole life. Just
ause you like different things than they do doesn't mean they're better than you
you're worse. You're just different, Peter. And you have to stand up and face
m."

Peter bit his lip and glanced at Lewis, who nodded back as if he agreed with

Peter let out a big sigh. "Okay. Let's try it."

37

Later I sat on the bench in the back of the dining hall with Peter and Lew

At my feet was Andy's one-million candle power SuperBeam flashlight, which

asked him to lend me along with the Cheese Whiz. As soon as the movie starte

Marty warned us not to get into any trouble, and left. Then the cool guys

disappeared.

"Ready?" I whispered to Peter and Lewis.

"I don't know," Peter whispered back nervously. "You sure this is a good

idea?"

"No," I whispered. "But can you think of anything better?"

Peter shook his head.

"Then let's do it," I said.

The crickets were chirping in the moonlight. Lewis, Peter, and I snuck

around the back of the cabins until we got to B-13. Inside the cabin we could h

whispers and the squeak of bedsprings as the cool guys set their booby traps.

Lewis and I opened our day packs, which we'd hidden behind the cabin

before going to the dining hall to see the movie. We took out rope and the cans

Cheese Whiz. Then Lewis and Peter got out their flashlights. I was already

carrying Andy's SuperBeam.

"Ready?" I whispered.

"Ready," Lewis replied.

We quietly snuck around to the front of the cabin. Inside the cool guys were still setting up their booby traps. But when the front door creaked, they looked up.

Click! Click! Click!

Lewis, Peter, and I flicked on our flashlights and aimed the beams right into their eyes. Lewis got Dan, Peter got Rick, and I got Zack with the SuperBeam. They all cowered, holding up their hands to block the bright light, squinting as they tried to see.

"Hey! What's going on?"

"Turn those things off!"

"Stop shining it in my eyes!"

We kept the flashlights on, blinding them, and didn't say a word.

"Who are you guys?" Dan asked.

I nudged Peter.

"Uh, we are the Dork Protection Posse," Peter said.

"What?"

"The Dork Protection Posse," Peter repeated.

"We protect dorks against those who seek to do them harm."

"Wait a minute." Zack straightened up. Even though the SuperBeam was still blinding him, he smiled. "I know who you are. You're Gummi Bear. And I bet your buddies are Sleeping Beauty and Mighty Mouse."

"The Dork Protection Posse, huh?" Dan said with a nasty grin.

Still shielding his eyes from the lights, Zack took a step toward us. "Isn't that cute?" he asked. "The Dork Protection Posse has come to protect the dork."

"Yeah," added Dan. "But who's gonna protect the Dork Protection Posse?"

They came toward us. Peter took a step back and glanced at me. "Now what?"

38

Zack and Dan were closing in on us. Peter, Lewis, and I backed toward the wall.

"I thought we were gonna get back up help," Peter said nervously.

"I thought so too," I said.

"So where is it?" Peter asked.

"Good question," I answered, glancing at Rick.

Dan and Zack were getting closer. We kept our flashlights on their faces, but it didn't stop them.

"This was a really great idea, Jake," Lewis muttered sarcastically.

"Hey, I only said we should try it, okay?" I shot back. "I never promised you it would work."

Meanwhile, Zack was rolling up the sleeves of his shirt. "I think the Dork Protection Posse is about to become the Dead Protection Posse."

"Yeah," said Dan. "Dead Meat."

They were only a few feet away now. I looked at Rick again. This time I caught his eye.

"Wait a minute, guys," Rick said.

Zack and Dan stopped. "What is it?" Zack asked.

"This is dumb," Rick said. "Somehow they found out we were playing a trick on them, so they decided to play a trick on us. I don't see why it has to turn into an all-out rumble."

"You chicken?" Zack sneered.

"No, I'm not chicken," Rick shot back. "I just don't see the point in hurting them. They didn't do anything to us."

"That's right," Zack said. "And now I'm gonna make sure they don't do anything to us."

It was time to make my move. I quickly muttered, "The bozo says, 'What?'"

"What?" Zack frowned.

Rick grinned.

"Come on, Rick," I said. "You know what I'm talking about."

The smile disappeared from Rick's face.

Zack stopped and looked back at Rick. "What's he talking about?"

"Peabrain says, 'What?' " I said.

"What?" Zack spun around and wrinkled his forehead.

Rick grinned again.

"It'll be four against two," I said to Rick.

"Huh?" Zack looked back and forth between us. "What's going on?"

Rick looked uncertain.

"Now I get it," Lewis whispered. "He's the back up?"

I nodded and looked at Rick. "Come on, man. This way they'll leave Peter

ne and we'll all have a decent month."

"What?" said Zack.

"That's what the veghead said," I said.

Rick grinned.

"Veghead?" Zack scowled.

"Hey, I get it!" Dan gasped. "The veghead says, 'What?'"

Zack turned. "What?"

"That's what the veghead said," Dan tried to explain.

Meanwhile, the rest of us rolled our eyes and grinned.

"The . . . veghead . . . says . . . 'What?'" Zack muttered to himself. Suddenly

eyes widened. "The bozo says, 'What?' . . . The bonehead says, 'What?'... The

brain says 'What?'"

He finally understood.

Zack grit his teeth, balled his hands into fists, and spun to face me. There

; murder in his eyes. "Why you ..."

I quickly looked at Rick. Now I *really* needed him. But Rick just gave me a

ny stare.

Zack came toward me, prepared to kill. I dropped the SuperBeam and rais

my fists. Next to me, Peter and Lewis did the same thing.

The only way we were going down was swinging. But against Dan and Z

we wouldn't have a chance.

"Hold it," Rick said.

Zack stopped. "Why?"

Rick walked around him and stood with Lewis, Peter, and me. "If you tak

on Jake, you take us all on."

Zack narrowed his eyes. "What's with you?"

"I'm just tired of you picking on people," Rick said. "You never pick on

anyone who'll fight back. I think that makes you the biggest chicken of all."

Zack sputtered and snarled, he cursed at us and said a lot of nasty stuff. B

Rick was right. When it was four against two, Zack didn't want to fight.

Later that night I stood by my bunk, speaking quietly to Rick and Lewis.

"Thanks, guys," I said. "It wouldn't have worked without you."

"I'm glad you got me to do it," Lewis said. "Otherwise, I probably would have just stuck to myself, thinking I was lucky they were picking on Peter and not me."

Rick nodded. "I know what you mean."

"Get in your bunks, guys," Marty said.

I got into bed feeling confident that I'd done the right thing. Although I was sort of disappointed that we didn't get to dangle Zack and Dan from the rafters and give them Super Cheese Whiz Wedgies.

I hadn't picked on Peter, and I hadn't protected him either. I'd helped him learn how to protect himself. That had to be the right thing to do. And hopefully it would be my ticket into the second day of camp, and to an okay time for the rest of the month.

Despite the lumpy pillow and itchy blanket, I slept soundly that night.

DAY FOUR

I felt a bump and opened my eyes. *Huh!? What was I doing on the bus again?*

We were pulling into the parking lot.

No! NO! NO!

Not again!

It couldn't be!

It wasn't fair!

"You can't do this to me!" I shouted angrily. "I did everything right! I did everything I possibly could! I've been *good!*"

Every head on the bus turned.

"You don't get it," I told them. "I've been here before. I've done this."

They all stared at me. A sea of frowns. They thought I was crazy.

I turned to Zack, Dan, and Rick in the back of the bus. "Zack, you're gonna pick on Peter today. You're gonna challenge him to one-handed, one-footed tetherball. You're gonna put plastic wrap on his glass so that the bug juice spills on him, and put detergent in his Water Pik. Dan, you're gonna go along with whatever Zack does because you're just a follower. Rick, you're gonna go along with Zack, too, even though you don't like it. Deep down inside you don't like picking on people, but you feel like you're stuck with Zack because it's important for you to be cool."

I turned to Lewis. "You're gonna stay out of it, Lewis. Zack's going to pick on you a little, but you're going to stand up to him."

"How do you know I have a Water Pik?" Peter asked from his seat.

"Believe me, I know," I said.

"What about Andy and me?" Josh asked.

"You guys aren't involved in this," I said. "Your cabins are on the other side of the athletic field. But hold onto your Cheeze Whiz and crackers. You're gonna need that stuff after you see what they serve for lunch."

Zack, Dan, and Rick gave me strange looks as they passed my seat and got off the bus.

Peter, Andy, and Josh were still looking at me like I'd lost my marbles.

Why was I still in the first day of camp?

What could I possibly have done wrong?

Lewis stood up and got off the bus, followed by Peter.

Now only Josh, Andy, and I were left on the bus. They stood up and slung their day packs over their shoulders.

"Aren't you getting off?" Andy asked.

And go through all that garbage again? I shook my head.

"You have to get off the bus, Jake," Josh said.

"No way," I said. "I'm not doing this again."

"You're not doing what again?" Andy asked.

There was no point in explaining. They wouldn't believe me, and it made no difference anyway.

But if I didn't get off the bus, then I wouldn't have to go through the first day of camp again.

"Uh, boys?" Down at the front of the bus Mr. Mailer had climbed back on. "Time to get off and get your bags."

I stayed seated. Andy and Josh gave me worried looks.

"Come on," Andy whispered urgently. "They want you off the bus."

I crossed my arms and shook my head. "No way."

"Come on, boys," Mr. Mailer said. "We need this bus."

"Jake, for the last time," Josh pleaded.

"Go on," I said. "Have a great camp experience."

Josh and Andy frowned at each other, then looked back at me.

"Are you serious?" Josh asked. "We wouldn't even be here if it weren't for you."

"Yeah, this whole thing was your idea," Andy said.

"I'm sure you'll have a great time," I said.

"Boys?" Mr. Mailer said. "Is something wrong?"

Josh turned to him. "Yeah, our friend Jake won't get off the bus."

The corners of Mr. Mailer's mouth fell. I doubt he needed this kind of
ravation on the first day of camp. He came down the aisle toward me.

"What's your name, son?" he asked.

I told him.

"We need this bus back," he said. "You have to get off."

"Listen, Mr. Mailer," I said. "I'm really sorry to do this to you, but there's no
 I'm getting off this bus."

42

Mr. Mailer talked to me for a long time. Then he got Marty to come talk to me.

Then they called the state police and got a trooper to come talk to me.

Then they called my parents and said they had to come get me.

Four hours later my dad got there. I was still sitting in the bus. Dad wasn't happy.

I put my duffle bag in our van and he drove me home.

"Why, Jake?" he asked on the way.

"I can't explain it, Dad," I said. "Just believe me. It has to be this way."

Dad shook his head and sighed. "Well, at least it was the first day. I can still get a refund."

We rode along in silence for a while. Then I remembered something.

"Hey, Dad, does Jessica know I'm coming home?"

"I don't see how she could," Dad replied. "She's over at the town pool, at work."

Good, I thought.

Later that afternoon I stood by the living room window and watched my sister come up the walk. Just as she reached the front door, I pulled it open.

"Ahhh!" she screeched. "Jake, what are you doing here?"

"I want my donuts," I growled.

"What!?" She stared at me in wide-eyed disbelief.

"You heard me. I want my donuts."

Her jaw dropped. "You . . . you came all the way home from camp to get your donuts?"

"Nobody takes my donuts."

"Are you crazy?"

"Just give me my donuts!"

"I... I can't," she stammered. "I ate them."

"Then I'm gonna cut them out of you." I went into the kitchen and came back with a dull butter knife.

When I got back to the front door, it was wide open. Jessica was running down the street as fast as she could.

That night I laid my head down on my nice soft feather pillow and pulled up my comfortable blanket. I couldn't remember being so glad to see my own bed.

After all, how can you be stuck in the first day of camp if you're not there?

43

DAY FIVE

I felt a bump and opened my eyes.

Oh, no! I was on the bus again.

This had to be some kind of joke.

A really bad, sick joke.

"Have a nice nap, Sleeping Beauty?" Zack asked.

Was there nothing I could do to get out of the first day of camp?

"What's the matter?" Zack asked. "Can't talk?"

But there had to be a way out. Last time it happened, when I was trapped in the first day of school, I'd figured out how to escape it.

That meant I was still doing something wrong.

I just had to figure out what it was.

"Hey, I'm talking to you," Zack said.

I had to think. I had to concentrate. I had to retrace my steps through the past four days. Somewhere in those days was the key, the missing link that would get me out of this mess.

"Hey," Zack said.

I looked up at him. "Bug off, wombat."

"Huh?" Zack started to make a fist.

"Lay off him," Rick said.

Zack glowered at me, but continued down the aisle and got off the bus.

Was I supposed to do something different with Peter? It didn't make sense. Somehow, deep inside, I knew that helping Peter learn to defend himself was the right thing to do.

But then why was I still trapped in the first day of camp? Was there someone else I had to help?

"Aren't you getting off?" Andy asked. He and Josh were standing with their day packs slung over their shoulders.

Did I really have to get off and go through it all again?

I guess I had to . . . until I figured out what to do.

That day I tried to do everything right.

I helped Peter learn to defend himself again.

I warned him about the plastic wrap.

I sailed with Lewis and got him to join the Dork Protection Posse.

I got Rick to take our side against Zack and Dan.

Finally, it was time to go to sleep.

I went into the bathroom and washed up.

I was halfway back to my bunk when I realized I'd forgotten to do something. It was something I'd forgotten to do every night since I'd gotten to camp.

But it couldn't be the answer, could it?

I wasn't going to take any chances.

I went back into the bathroom ... and brushed my teeth.

44

DAY SIX

I felt a bump and opened my eyes.

I was on the bus again.

I was going through the first day of camp again!

I was going to look at American Chop Suey again!

"No! No!" I screamed.

I couldn't take it!

Everyone stared at me. I didn't care. I jumped out of my seat and ran to the
ıt of the bus.

"Hey!" the driver shouted as I grabbed the wheel and jammed my foot
inst the gas pedal, flooring it.

Varrroooom! The bus's wheels spun wildly, spraying gravel around the
king lot. The bus lurched forward. Outside campers and counselors dove out of
way.

"Hey! What's he doing?" "Stop!" "Look out!" Inside the bus kids screamed
ve hurtled over a log barrier and caromed across the grass toward the lake.

"You're gonna kill us all!" the bus driver shouted as we grappled over the
ering wheel.

"I don't care!" I screamed. "I— "

"Hey, Jake, wake up!" Someone was shaking my shoulder. "Jake?"

I opened my eyes.

I was lying in my camp bunk. Marty, Peter, and Lewis were staring down me. Marty's hand was on my shoulder.

"You okay?" he asked.

The sun was shining outside. The air had a fresh chilly morning smell. Despite my lumpy pillow and itchy blanket, I felt warm and cozy.

"Where am I?" I asked.

"Camp Walton," Marty said.

"What day is it?" I asked.

"The second day of camp," said Lewis.

"You must've had a bad dream," added Peter.

I sat up and rubbed my eyes.

"You okay now?" Marty asked.

"Uh ... yeah ... I guess." I nodded.

Was it possible?

Had I really gotten out of the first day of camp!?

Marty clapped his hands together. "Okay, guys, get your swimsuits on."

"What're you talking about?" Zack asked. "We haven't had breakfast yet."

"In this cabin we always take a nice cold swim in the lake before breakfast," Marty announced. "Come on, guys, let's go."

Everyone groaned.

I pulled my blanket up to my chin, dreading the thought of swimming in that freezing cold lake. If only I could be trapped in the first day of camp again!

END

Made in the USA
Coppell, TX
22 November 2020